M000317103

This novel is a collection of poems as the author wrestles and grapples with difficult concepts in an abstract, creative way, while maintaining a story line. The mission with this novel is to end human suffering for everyone because the author suffered a lot growing up. Despite the tragedies the author faces, this novel is very powerful.

Tyler Harrison

I Couldn't Find Her So I Created Her

Wrestling with new concepts, I got them from downstairs

AUSTIN MACAULEY PUBLISHERS™

LONDON · CAMBRIDGE · NEW YORK · SHARJAH

Ordering Information:
Quantity sales: special discounts are available on quantity purchases by corporations, associations, and others. For details, contact the publisher at the address below.

Publisher's Cataloguing-in-Publication data
Harrison, Tyler
I Couldn't Find Her So I Created Her

ISBN 9781645361008 (Paperback)
ISBN 9781645361015 (Hardback)
ISBN 9781645365891 (ePub e-book)

Library of Congress Control Number: 2020902896

www.austinmacauley.com/us

First Published (2020)
Austin Macauley Publishers LLC
40 Wall Street, 28th Floor
New York, NY 10005
USA

mail-usa@austinmacauley.com
+1 (646) 5125767

God is alive, God gave me life, God is living on the inside, God is the reason that I'm still alive. Just thankful I get to operate and participate on this place called Earth. Thankful for all the ones that were good to me, and if you weren't, I forgive you too.

My nana is a wise woman; she was an editor for the *Eufaula* newspaper and also was an antique dealer when she worked. She is an intelligent woman, and I love both of my grandparents very much. My grandpa travelled a lot; he was a regional manager for AGCO, which was a company that distributed agriculture equipment. Because of them, my brothers and I had Christmas every year and still continue to get blessed with Christmas by them. We got to go on fun road trips after I turned 12, with my grandpa. Because of them I got to experience the beach for the first time and a handful of times afterward. Very thankful for all that they have done for myself and my brothers. Yesterday on 5-27-2019 they celebrated 52 years of marriage, how beautiful. I love them. Thankful to God for them…

God is alive, God gave me life, God is living on the inside, God is the reason that I'm still alive. Just thankful I get to operate and participate on this place called Earth. Thankful for all the ones that were good to me, and if you weren't, I forgive you too.

My nana is a wise woman; she was an editor for the *Eufaula* newspaper and also was an antique dealer when she worked. She is an intelligent woman, and I love both of my grandparents very much. My grandpa travelled a lot; he was a regional manager for AGCO, which was a company that distributed agriculture equipment. Because of them, my brothers and I had Christmas every year and still continue to get blessed with Christmas by them. We got to go on fun road trips after I turned 12, with my grandpa. Because of them I got to experience the beach for the first time and a handful of times afterward. Very thankful for all that they have done for myself and my brothers. Yesterday on 5-27-2019 they celebrated 52 years of marriage, how beautiful. I love them. Thankful to God for them…

Before you read my story, I want you to know that the autobiography, where I tell about my life and Lucy's life is based on a true story. The only thing that isn't true is that I changed her name and she is a creative writing major instead of a film artist/director. I am not writing this story so you can feel sorry for me, I am writing it because I believe my story needs to be heard so I can impact millions of people's lives for the liberation of others. I forgive anyone who has ever hurt me or wronged me in any way. I want to end human suffering for everyone because I have known suffering throughout my life, but there's one thing that covers it all which is love. Loving and Serving are the two most phenomenal things we can all do to make the world a better place. I also am a Christian and I am not perfect but I can tell you all this, that each and every one of us has greatness and has a purpose! (NIV)

"Bear with each other and forgive one another if any of you has a grievance against someone. Forgive as the Lord forgave you."

Colossians 3:13

"Do not judge and you will not be judged. Do not condemn, and you will not be condemned. Forgive, and you will be forgiven."

Luke 6:37

"Whoever conceals their sins does not prosper, but the one who confesses and renounces them, finds mercy."

Proverbs 28:13

"Therefore, my friends, I want you to know that through Jesus the forgiveness of sins is proclaimed to you. Through him, everyone who believes is set free from every sin, a justification you were not able to obtain under the Law of Moses."

Acts 13:38-39
Romans 8:38-39

"For I am convinced that neither death nor life, neither angels nor demons, [a] neither the present nor the future, nor any powers, 39 neither height nor depth, nor anything else in all creation, will be able to separate us from the love of God that is in Christ Jesus our Lord."

John 8

But Jesus went to the Mount of Olives.

At dawn he appeared again in the temple courts, where all the people gathered around him, and he sat down to teach them. The teachers of the law and the Pharisees brought in a woman caught in adultery. They made her stand before the group and said to Jesus, "Teacher, this woman was caught in the act of adultery. In the Law Moses commanded us to stone such women. Now what do you say?" They were using this question as a trap, in order to have a basis for accusing him.

But Jesus bent down and started to write on the ground with his finger. When they kept on questioning him, he straightened up and said to them, "Let any one of you who is without sin be the first to throw a stone at her." Again he stooped down and wrote on the ground.

At this, those who heard began to go away one at a time, the older ones first, until only Jesus was left, with the woman still standing there. Jesus straightened up and asked her,

"'Woman, where are they? Has no one condemned you?'

'No one, sir,' she said.

'Then neither do I condemn you,' Jesus declared. 'Go now and leave your life of sin.'"

Romans 10:9

If you declare with your mouth, "Jesus is Lord," and believe in your heart that God raised him from the dead, you will be saved.

I met her as I walked outside the mall, as her eyes caught mine my heart began to fall, as I talked to her I had to make a call, between getting her number and letting her go. For moments like this are made for stories to be told, this is the story of how she stole my heart as we journeyed down the road. So, I asked her what your plans are for tonight. For a woman as lovely as you should be treasured by and by. For if you're searching for a good time, don't be afraid, put your hand in mine, for unconditional love starts one day at a time. I'm the finest of them all, but you shimmer brighter than fall. You can find me every day after class, reading in the study hall. For John Greene's TFIOS is my favorite of them all. He is an author and I am as well. Have you ever been to a formal ball, where lovers dance? Since we're of age to drink, we won't break the law.

She asked me, "What's your name?"

I replied, "Tyler."

As we walked down the road, she smiled and replied saying, "I like the way you rhyme, the way you connect words in a matter of lines, the way you capture my soul when your hands in mine, and the way the butterflies fly when I'm looking in your eyes. For my name is Lucy, I'm a film artist and director, I shoot movies. I have even shot movies that play at the movies. For capturing moments, there is something so moving, as touching the spirit, like in romance movies."

"Wow, how cool," I replied, "I appreciate the kind words and I sound like your guy! Let me get your number and join me for dinner. I'll pick you up at five. I'll love listening to you. Tell me about your life and for when the days get hard we will be alright."

She replied, "Only, if only you don't lose your grip when your hands get tired."

Thirty minutes to five, thoughts are running wild, I was pretty brave earlier now I feel like hiding, see it's not easy for me to let someone in, for when I was a child, it was natural to run and hide, to cope with the pain inside, of watching my brothers and mom screaming from the pain, we would cry, helpless and shy. I always kept quiet, my father was the culprit. He caused the numbing in my eyes. Now that I'm older, I'm a lot bolder, I got stronger shoulders after three years of losing my way, and I'm finally sober. Prayed for wisdom as a child didn't know it meant, I would have gone through the coldest. I know it sounds crazy but I'm thankful for the storms, didn't know we would be torn. Thankful I'm still alive, to tell you all that it's okay to want to run and hide, it's okay to not be alright, it's okay to launch out of the darkest nights, it's okay to search for your purpose under the light. See, God gives his hardest battles to his strongest soldiers. Gave me the ability to write, he gave me the ability to rhyme, he gave me the gift of life, now that I'm grown, chasing this passion of mine, doing hair and speaking into this mic, to set all your souls free while you all are saving mine. My greatest joy comes from serving, the secret to happiness is loving, if your searching for passion, the most satisfying life is in our ultimate effort of saving lives. Rescuing these people from the hate and the violence, reaching out to these victims who weren't sure if there was anyone fighting for them. See, when I was 16, I tried to speak out about my dad. I tried to reach out. I gave all I had, he tried to put me in a mental hospital for going mad, I had enough, but I kept quiet, didn't want to be in a hospital broken and sad for just wanting to tell the truth, I kept it all in. It wasn't until I woke up to go use the restroom, but as soon as I opened the door, I lost my breath, it was my older brother, Clayton getting strangled by my dad. His face turned purple, I said, please put my brother down. He did slowly, I thought I was going to lose Clayton that day, he was going to kill him if I wouldn't have walked in to save him. It's incredible how little moments can change so many things. After that our dad left on his motorcycle, I called the cops we made a police report and I told my mom that I was finished, that if she didn't leave him that my brothers and I are going to live with the State of Alabama. She finally gained the strength to leave him and we went and lived in a homeless shelter in Cullman, I was now in 10th grade about to turn 17. Someone tell me how to feel for now that I'm older. I can see who is real, this is more than a drill. I'm searching for the love that will last longer than a pill. I just pulled up to her house, my eyes water as she opens the door.

I put the car in drive and we pull out of her drive, "Are you okay she asks?" I replied, "Excuse me if I'm a little emotional right now, I haven't dated in a year. I have been focused on Cosmetology school and coming to peace with my past."

"What do you mean coming to peace with your past?"

This was the part where I could let her see me for who I really am, or I could put on another mask, but see if I mask my problems with her she will never see me for who I really am. She will never be able to help me stand.

"You seem like a strong girl," I replied, "from the glimmer of your eyes, the sparkle, and shine, I know you can withstand what I'm about to tell you and it is okay to breakdown and cry. You may want to press record before I start. See it's a miracle that I'm here for before I came into this world, I almost lost my life, my dad would constantly fight with my mother, physically and verbally. Well while my mother was pregnant with me, my dad pushed my mom off a five-foot porch, luckily by the grace of God she landed on her feet. My father worked for a lawn business at the time. One day when he came home, my mother said to him that God told her that he was doing things he shouldn't have been doing. He was guilty of having a stash of porn magazines that he would go through at work. He denied it and proceeded to slap my mom in the face out of rage. Lucy, let me fast forward a couple of years, my father joins the military, he got stationed in Texas, I was six years old at the time, the physical and verbal abuse among my two brothers and mom happened my entire childhood growing up. He put his hands on me a few times growing up, but I suffered most when I watched my family suffer for I was helpless and there wasn't anything I could do. My father would drink alcohol every day when he got home from work. I had witnessed him chasing my mother around the house, picking her up with one arm as he choked her, throwing her down, sometimes she would outrun him and lock herself in the car. At night sometimes, she would sleep in the car even if it was freezing outside, she would crank the car up ever so she could feel the warmth of the heat. As a child I was very frightened to witness all of this, I've seen my mom get hit, choked out, her hair pulled by my dad. My brother, Clayton was my dad's other favorite person to torture. For some reason, he didn't start with me till I was older, maybe because I decided to fight back. My father would bend him over the couch and beat him over the couch like a madman, all I could do was helplessly watch as my brother screamed for help. I wanted to stop the suffering, but I didn't know how to. He would threaten us telling us we better not tell anyone what happens at home. My dad did four tours in Iraq, my happiest times as a child was when he was away on his tours. When he was gone, no physical or mental abuse was happening, it was bonding time with my brothers and mom. We spent a lot of time skateboarding, roller-skating, play wrestling, and playing video games. Our mother would cook the most delicious meals from tacos to spaghetti, to Cajun stir-fry chicken with white rice. When our dad got back from the war, I remember him drinking a lot with our neighbor, David, our dad called up his parents and cussed his parents out for not letting him get a job with the company our Papa worked for. He was furious and ripped his shirt off, ended up driving drunk and got a DUI, then it was even more hell for us because he was angry that he couldn't drive for six months and had to have our mom drive him everywhere. Fast forward to 2008, I am now 12 years old my dad is getting put out of the military after nine years, the doctor said, he wasn't mentally capable to be a Sergeant anymore and be responsible for soldiers. He also diagnosed him with Post Traumatic Stress Disorder. My brothers and mom were born in Jasper Alabama, my dad was conceived in Cullman then given up for adoption, so our parents made the decision that we were going to move to Cullman, Alabama. We moved into a two-bedroom, one-bathroom, mobile home at the national mobile home disposal in Vinemont, in Cullman County. My brother Clayton was still very joyful and silly, our dad did not like this because if he wasn't happy no one could be happy. Well, he took his pair of hair clippers and held my brother, Clayton down on the floor by the back of his neck and shaved his head bald. I was finishing up my 5th grade year at Vinemont Elementary at the time. We were moving to the city in three to four months, I went to West Elementary. Mrs. White was my homeroom teacher, but I had Mrs. Rackstraw for English. It was in her class that I discovered, I could write poetry. Never will I forget that moment with my soul, brain, and body clicked with words. I still have all the poems I wrote when I was in her class. Fast forward to 7th grade, I was coming home from football practice, I walk up the stairs at our apartment at Oak Manor and my dad started choking me as soon as I made it up the steps. Fast forward to 9th grade, I pierced my ears, my dad didn't like them, I refused to take them out and so he ripped them out. I walked out of the house, I was so hurt crying walking down the road, my mom had come after me, talked with me then led me back to the house. Let me take you to the 10th grade. I woke up to go use the restroom, as I opened the door my brother, Clayton was floating in the air fighting for his next breath, he almost died his face was as purple as a plum. I said, please put my brother down. After that, I told my mom, I couldn't live here anymore. I literally watched my brother's soul almost leave his body. I called the cops, but our mom didn't press charges this was in 2012. We did pack up what we could and went to stay in a homeless shelter in Cullman. We stayed there for three weeks then we moved into a one-bedroom apartment. All four of us, yes it was a little cramped, but the peace of mind was worth it all. Our mother got a job at Walmart here in town. After a month, we move into a two-bedroom apartment at the village east. Six months later, we move into an apartment at the Cullman Housing Authority. We all are very happy. Our mom ends up starting a dating website, she knows the guy for a month then moves us all in with him, a couple of months go by bobby wants to kick Clayton out, our mom is so in love with bobby that she is ready for him to rule her life, she agrees to kick Clayton out to the streets. Another couple of months go by he wants to kick Preston and me out it is Christmas of 2014; our mom wouldn't let him kick us out. I had got my GED and just spent a year in the National Guard, by this time. We all ended up going back to the homeless shelter in Cullman, we were there for a week and bobby got in touch with our mom. Our mom ends up leaving me and my brother standing there on the street as bobby's mom picks her up and takes her to Fayette County. He wouldn't let us stay there so we were stranded with both of our parents out of the question. Preston called up his tutor in Cullman and he took Preston in. For me, I had no choice but to serve more time in hell at my dad's house. Clayton was running the streets with our cousin getting lost in his mind to cope and deal with the abuse that we took on. I enroll at Wallace State and start taking basic courses not sure about what I want to be. I bought a 2001 VW Jetta as my first car. School went great during my first year then I started partying and losing my way to cope and deal with the pain as well. A year passes, it is Thanksgiving of 2015. Our dad had made a new girlfriend that lived in Oakman. Her daughter, Savannah, loved kingdom hearts and the fault in our stars, so we hit it off pretty good as well. Preston was visiting with us, well it was a day before Thanksgiving and our dad invites us to ride with him to Dollar General, Preston was full of joy being silly and our dad was uptight and angry, he told Preston to stay in the car after he invited us to the store. Preston was like yeah right, I'm not staying in the car, so he got out and by the time he got to the door at Dollar General, he came up behind Preston, put him in a headlock and dragged him across the parking lot then physically put him in the car. The women in Dollar General were freaking out."

She said, "Did that really just happened?"

"I was trying to remain calm and I said he wanted him to stay in the car and then we continued shopping. Our mom was 20 minutes away, so we had our dad drive us to Fayette County. When we got there, I called Savannah and let her know what happened and to please stay away from our dad that he is dangerous. Rene was our adopted grandpa, we adopted him, and well he came to pick us up a week later. I had to go back to hell to my dad's house. One thing that I left out from my childhood when I was younger was that my brothers and I were molested by our cousin, he was 14 and I was four when it happened. Clayton was six and Preston was one year old. He said, we were going to play hide and seek, it was very shocking for me it was very traumatic. I didn't know what was going on but he took my brothers and myself in the bedroom, said we were going to play hide and seek then shut the door. He took our clothes off and did stuff to us, I can replay him saying come on we're going to play hide and seek. I remember laying on all fours on the carpet. I still remember how it felt, you are the first person I have talked to about this in ten years. Our cousin later ended up in juvenile. I'm not sure how long he stayed in juvenile, we also had to go to counseling for it. Someone had molested my cousin, so I guess he thought it was normal to do that to other people, but it definitely scared me and my brothers. I have told you about my life behind closed doors now. I will take you from the beginning of my childhood and tell you about my life away from the house. So I grew up in Killeen, Texas from age six to 12. I attended school at Hay Branch Elementary and I lived in Summer-field Mobile home Park. It was in kindergarten that I was introduced to reading, I was afraid, I was never going to learn how to read. I even got held back in kindergarten because of that. After two years of kindergarten, something powerful took place in my mind, I had an Aha moment, right before my eyes my brain was dissecting and connecting words and sentences. During 1st-grade, I was very hyper and had trouble focusing so my mom got me an appointment with the doctor and he diagnosed me along with my brothers with ADHD. He prescribed concerta to me. It helped tremendously. I was able to follow along with the teachers to learn in class. I was six when I started playing Kingdom Hearts, I love Kingdom Hearts. It is a game where you travel to different worlds, fighting the darkness alongside with Disney Characters. This is the story of the tortoise and the hare played out through my life. I hope you enjoy; everyone has the potential for greatness! I started playing an MMORPG game in 2nd-grade it was called Runescape. I would play this game alongside my best friends and brothers. My close friends were Nicholas Fletcher, Michael Barrios, Phillip File, Nichole File, and Jacob Warren. Nichole was Phillip's sister. She and I would go roller-skating outside after school a lot growing up at Summer-field. It was in 3rd grade when I was introduced to multiplication, I loved math when I was younger, and I made up my mind to be the best at the multiplication tables. I wasn't great at them, to begin with, but I put in the work, and the work paid off. The teachers had organized events for us where we would have competitions with the other classes. Well, I ended up beating all of the other classes and as a reward, we received a day where we could be what we wanted to wear. We had to wear uniforms to school. I spent a lot of my time after school skateboarding with my brothers, also on Runescape I would chop willow trees, cook, and fish with my friends Nicholas and Michael. Josh Abrams was one of our neighbors, well one day he and Clayton had found some cans of green spray paint and they chose to paint the playground. Our mom and Josh's mom were very unhappy with their behavior, they had to clean up the mess that Josh and Clayton created. Jaiden was one of our friends too he was special, he liked to play with peoples' feet. Every time he would come over, he would ask our mom if he could play with her feet. One day, I was riding the bus home, we made multiple stops, well at this particular stop my friend, Rashad was getting off of the bus and he tripped getting off of the bus, hitting his head on the steps of the bus while messing up his leg. Also, there was a boy who sat behind us on the bus named Dominique, my little brother would chant his name, Dominique, Dominique, Dominique! There was one boy, named Javion. He saw that my brother, Clayton wore hearing aids so he started flicking his ears, Clayton turned around took his foot and shoved it in Javion's face, kicking him over and over again. Clayton did not have the patience for that kid being ugly towards him. I had a crush on Bailey Cotton from the moment I saw her in 1st grade till it was my last time seeing her when I was in the 5th grade. She never noticed me though, I was the geeky intelligent guy that you would call a nerd, but I take pride in my intelligence for it makes me aware of things people are blinded by. Mrs. Perry was my favorite teacher at Hay Branch Elementary. My favorite day of the year every year was field day. I loved it when it was Christmas time too when Santa would come to the office at the mobile home park. It was in 2008 when I first created my YouTube account. I fell in love with music videos and so I had dreams of creating my own which I acted on a couple of years later, I had desires to not only entertain people but to change their life to show people that they really can be what they want to be. Our mom would take us to the church at Grace Christian Center, I loved going there. My brothers and I would also go skateboarding at a downhill park in Texas, it was near the civic center, when I was in the 5th-grade I made a great friend, and his name was Blake Woken. My brother, Clayton went to school with his brother, Alix Woken and became good friends with him as well. We would also go skateboarding on base since Blake's dad was in the military and my brothers, all of us would go to Round Rock Texas to skate at the skate-park there. My brothers, mom, and I would spend time at Mary Richardson's house. Tommy was one of her sons that we would hang out with. We would go to the Killeen mall, Chick-Fil-A and Ryan's a good bit to eat. One Halloween, Tommy bought a Slipknot mask and wore it around the mall while getting candy. The mask was so offensive that a security guard had asked him to take it off. I would also spend time at Conner Berg's house, we would go skateboarding together as well. One night, I stayed the night over and we built a fortress full of pillows and blankets it was very intricate. We watched Monster House and had buttery delicious popcorn, what an incredible time. I'm not sure if you are picking up on my patterns but I did my best to not be at home to always be with my friends because they guarded my heart. I stayed the night at Blake Woman's house and he showed me, Dawn of the Dead, that is where my love for zombie movies began. In February of 2008, I moved from Killeen, Texas to Cullman, Alabama. I was born in Jasper but Cullman was my new hometown. I finished my 5th grade year at Vinemont Elementary, the next year our parents moved us to Cullman City Schools. I was in 6th grade and I went to West Elementary, I really liked it there. My friends were Cole Brown, Grayson Webster, and Conner Pruitt. We were the crew, the outcasts of the school, the punk rockers who had a love for skateboarding and rock music. Grayson and I would sing while Cole played drums and Conner played guitar. We would go to Conner's house sometimes and jam out. We were ourselves if you were searching for normal, that wasn't us! I was still in choir ever since 1st grade, Mr. Clemmons was my music teacher he was phenomenal! My homeroom teacher was Mrs. White.

She was a great teacher as well. I enjoyed Mrs. Rakestraw's class very much because that is where I discovered that I could write! The next year, I was onto Cullman Middle School, I loved this because we got issued laptops! I only got to spend one semester at CMS because it was time to move again sadly. This time we were moving to Holly Pond which was a city that was still in Cullman County. People weren't very nice at Holly Pond. I weighed 220 pounds and was dealing with a toxic life at home and school, eating was my way of escaping while I coped through reality. A couple of months go by, I am tired of coming home crying myself to sleep because I hated my life during that time I just wanted to be loved and to connect with people. It was spirit week one week there, well it was pajama day and as I was walking back from lunch Josh Chambers and Dakota Haynes pull my pants down from behind me. I still hadn't hit puberty all the way so it was pretty embarrassing for myself, it didn't help that a ton of girls was watching as that happened. I decided to start working out, I spent every day after school running on the elliptical at the aquatic center, running for 40 minutes every day! After four months, I was down to 180 pounds, I had dropped 40 pounds. After a few months, our parents moved us back to Cullman City Schools. I tried out for the Cullman Bearcat football; Coach Turner gave me the position of offensive line as a right guard. Coach Turner and Coach Duke really shaped us into being the best. Spring training was a good way of setting discipline in us Mr. Agnew was my music teacher at CMS every other week was performance day where we could pick a song to sing and stand in front of the music class to sing. I would also hang out with Justin Woods, we would go skateboarding from his house to Sportsman's lake, we would skate around the lake as well, and when we were finished we would go to Jamie Bradley's house and hang out with her and Tiffany Smith. I loved going to every football game as a Cullman Bearcat football player! I loved Cullman City Schools, when we won it was great but when we lost it wasn't very gratifying! Defeat is not a good feeling at all but we always could learn something from our knockdowns! After my 8th-grade year, our parents decided it was time to move again, we were moving back to Vinemont. I was extremely upset about moving again. I fell into a depression where I stayed in the house all summer in my bedroom and just played video games every day. I gained 63 pounds. I was weighing 243 pounds after the summer was over, it was the most, I had ever weighed. When school started back, the first couple of weeks it was okay but it got worse. I didn't see my friends from Cullman anymore, I had lost my confidence from gaining so much weight, I had let myself go and people treated me the way I carried myself, like crap. I did make some friends at Vinemont they were: Blake Kimbril, Isaac Yarbrough, Duncan Hopper, Allison Fowler, Grace Griggs, Rodrigo, Rolando Ramon, Hannah Johnson, Edwin, and Cristobal. I rebelled against my parents. I was upset that they kept moving me to different schools. I decided not to do my schoolwork anymore. I would first sign my name on each assignment then turn it in. It came down to a point the principal would have me sit in a room all by myself and I would just sit in the room for eight hours every single day, they would isolate me like I was an alien or something. I was only hurting myself by not going with the system but I didn't want to play anymore. A couple of months go by, the school year was coming to an end, I had pierced my ears for the first time, my dad told me to take them out but I didn't so he ripped them out of my ears. Vinemont also sent me to alternative school a few times for my refusal to do the schoolwork. My favorite teacher at Vinemont was Mr. Heaton, he was the agriculture teacher. He was so funny while always having a positive impact on my brother and me. It was great to get withdrawn from Vinemont, I was moving back to Cullman for my 10th grade year. I had failed all my 9th grade courses but Cullman let me take 10th grade classes as long as I would go to Summer School after my 10th grade school year. My friends at Cullman would call me by T Harrison, this is when I spent a lot of time after school with my brothers making YouTube videos, my classmates loved my YouTube videos I was the sensation! This was when our mom left our dad and we were living in the homeless shelter. I made AB honor roll all year long at Cullman. One day during Physical Education, we went bowling, bowling went great. I had a great time with my friends! When we got ready to go, I was putting up my bowling ball, I had it in my left arm I tripped on one of the steps and the bowling ball landed on my right pinky breaking it in two places and I had to get 12 stitches. I was laying on the ground as blood was flowing out from my pinky like a waterfall, the coaches wrapped my pinky up for me till the ambulance got there to pick me up. When I got to the emergency room, the doctor stitched me up and wrapped me up, when I was finished a couple of days later, I had an appointment with the bone doctor to get an X-ray afterward he wrapped me in a cast. When 10th grade was finished, I was signed up for Summer School. I went two days. I couldn't stand the teacher not being there to teach the material and I was tired of my parents moving me around so I dropped out of high school. I took my GED test two weeks later and I passed it, then I went to the Army National Guard Office to sign up to join the military. My recruiter was Ashley Marta. She was a wonderful woman. Since I had only my GED so I had to take the TAPAS, AIMS, and ASVAB test and pass all of them I passed the ASVAB with flying colors but the other tests took me a little while to pass. I went down to MEPS three times before I even swore into the Guard. I may have fallen many times but I always get back up. I never gave up because I kept on trying regardless of the circumstances I was born into. It was September 30th, 2013 when I swore into the Army National Guard. I was so pumped, excited, my life had a new meaning. I was finally a part of something larger than myself, it was phenomenal! Now that I was in I would spend one weekend a month in the recruitment sustainment program where our recruiters would prepare us for basic held at the Armory in Oneonta. I trained every single day for basic. I had my run days and I had my muscle training days. On my run days, I would run two miles as fast as I could, on the muscle training days I would do 150 pushups and multiple sets of flutter kicks. My ship date for basic training was June 30th, so I spent eight months preparing for the day where my life would change. It was my ship date and I hugged my brothers, told them I loved them. I called up my best friend, Austin Thompson. I let them all know that I loved them. I told them, I will see you all on the other side, so I went to MEPS, from there I went to the airport, flew to Atlanta then flew to St. Louis Missouri, afterward I caught a bus to Fort Leonard Wood. My first couple of days there I was in reception with a lot of other future soldiers that were about to start basic. Reception was a place where you get analyzed, your physical, your shots, your uniforms, and personal hygiene items that you will use during basic. It was during reception that the eye doctors discovered that I had an eye disease, called Pars planitis but they still signed off for me to start basic. **Pars planitis** is a disease of the eye that is characterized by inflammation of the narrowed area (pars plana) between the colored part of the eye (iris) and the choroid. This may lead to blurred vision; dark, floating spots in the vision; and progressive vision loss. As the condition advances, cataracts, retinal detachment, or macular edema (fluid within the retina) may develop. Pars planitis, most often affects young men and is generally not associated with any other disease or symptoms (idiopathic); however, it can be associated with other autoimmune conditions such as multiple sclerosis and sarcoidosis. Treatment typically includes corticosteroid drugs, immunosuppressive medications, and/or surgery[1].

After the reception, we were introduced to the company where we would spend the next 20 weeks. My Military Occupational Specialty was 31 Bravo Military Police so I was going to an O.S.U.T (One Station Unit Training) where basic and AIT (Advanced Individual Training) which is the job training after basic is combined together at one unit. My company was Bravo 795 and I was in the third platoon, we were the Hellhounds! On my first day when basic started,

---

[1] https://rarediseases.info.nih.gov/diseases/7339/pars-planitis.

our drill sergeants picked us up in cattle carts like were cows or something, I found that very humorous! They blindfolded us so we couldn't see how to get to our company, once we got there, it was move private get the fuck off of the cart! Move it now!

As soon as I got off the cart, I heard, "Front lean and rest position move, in cadence, exercise."

This is known as the push-up. They smoked us for a good half hour then introduced themselves. We then entered our building and we were having lunch, we got our plate then we had to stand by our chair.

When everyone got their plate the drill sergeant said, "Sit."

We all took a deep breath in.

Then he said, "Down."

We all responded in unison, "Yes, drill, sergeant, moving drill, sergeant."

When we sat down we had to sit with our back straight up eating as fast as we could almost like robots. During my first three weeks there, we had shower drills, we had to countdown from 15 seconds that was all that we got for showers. In the mornings, we got 30 seconds to brush our teeth and shave our face, it was the most humbling experience I have taken on before. Our 4th week in training we started Basic Rifle Marksmanship. I enjoyed shooting but I couldn't see that well. I had blurs in my vision and it wasn't correctable with a lens even though I was issued a lens. I completed all of the basic training but I didn't pass the rifle range. Our last week, we were doing pushups when we went down we had to yell out I am, and when we pushed up we had to say an individual. That phrase really got me thinking maybe I am too much of an individual for the military, maybe there is something out there I really need to be doing. After basic, I spent three weeks and RHU which was the discharge unit. I called it, RHU resorts because we could sleep all day if we wanted too. I made some great friends there; Charlie Larabee, Jessie Gonzalez, and Timmy Beacham. Timmy would always take up for me when other people were rude to me, he had a good heart. It was my day, you never knew when you were going home they would call out names every day. Well, today they called my name, it was time to go home, home sweet home. I was so ready, I was going to have my brother, Clayton pick me up so I could surprise the family. He picked me up with one of our friends, Travis Lance but he wasn't the greatest guy to be hanging around.

Clayton said, "I love you, Tyler it is great to see you."

I replied, "I love you too, brother!"

We went to Welti Falls, we walked down the trail for about five minutes. It was nighttime.

Clayton pulled a blunt, rolled with marijuana, and I had never smoked it before he asked, "Do you want to take a few puffs, Tyler?"

I said, "Sure."

He lit it up, took a few puffs, passed it to Travis, then he passed it to me. I took two full draws of it and before I knew it I was about to fall to the ground. I had one arm on Clayton and Travis, they helped me walk to the car then I got in the backseat. Travis was driving, Clayton wanted to use my phone I didn't mind he had it longer than five minutes.

I said, "Clayton give me my phone."

He wouldn't so I started crying. I was hallucinating and after all the trauma from basic. I wept for hours. Clayton took me to Miss Sherri's house and I cried and told her about my basic experience, she was Clayton's godmother. The next day, I went to Berry where our mom lived, I knocked on the door, she was so happy to see me! She was still married to Bobby sadly. It was great seeing her again, getting to spend time with her. The next day, I went to go see Preston and my Dad this was right before thanksgiving right before our dad choked out Preston and drug him across the parking lot. Preston told me that it is getting worse over there since I have been gone. I could see the pain in his eyes, it was very sad. So much I wanted to do but I didn't know how to. This was the journey of me losing myself began, Travis and Clayton wanted to go on a road trip to Washington State to see my friend, Blake at the time. First I had to get some tattoos, buy a car, buy some weed, then we hit the road. We went in Clayton's car it was a 2005 Toyota Corolla, we were so excited but so reckless. After 1000 miles on the road we were in Denver Colorado, we stopped at the Walmart there to see if we could find someone to buy some weed from since it was legal in Colorado. We did, we bought seven grams, rolled up a blunt, lit it up then it was back on the road. We made it to Washington, Clayton and Travis only stayed for a couple of hours. I ended up staying with Blake. I stayed in Olympia for three weeks after that I was ready to come home, my Grandpa, Harrison flew me home, I am very thankful and grateful for my Grandparents, they have helped my family financially my whole life growing up. Our dad wouldn't buy us Christmas so our grandparents bought us Christmas every year. I am sure, they won't be happy about me telling my story but this is something I must do. When I got home, I registered for college classes. I had just got home a week or two before Thanksgiving. I was signed up for general study courses. My first semester in college went great. I took Math 098, Eng. 101, Art Appreciation, and Computer Applications where the teacher taught us how to use Microsoft Office. In my 2nd semester, I took in the summer of 2015. I was registered for a speech class with Mr. Metcalf. I came into class wearing blue jeans and a tank top showing off all of my tattoos. We all had to stand up and introduce ourselves, there was a pretty blonde girl in the class. I didn't remember her name until I saw that she added me on Facebook. We spent three to four weeks dating and I had ended up getting her pregnant. Well after she found out, she started being distant. I had a feeling she was seeing someone else. She was seeing Chris in class. She wanted to meet to talk to me about things so she borrowed Chris's car and came to talk to me in the parking lot in school. I stood there in the road as she pulled up. She rolled down the window, as I stood there thinking about what I was going to say, and how I was going to say it. I was numb. She blew the horn, waking me from my slumber.

I walked up to the car. I said, "What do you want Mariah?"

She replied, "It's about the baby. Are you going to come to the doctor's appointments with me?"

I yelled, "No, Mariah! I will see the baby when he gets here!"

I was wrong for reacting that way. I was so upset over the whole situation. I kissed her then I went to my tattoo shop with my best friend, Austin. I was completely broken during that time going through that with Mariah. My tattoo shop was in Jasper, it was expert ink and my tat artist was Clint Chappell. I got the word Dreamer tatted on me because I am a dreamer. I was going to raise my son to be a dreamer, and I wanted to name him, Dreamer Cole like Dreamer's Code for there is a code to being a Dreamer. The code of having an open mind to all things is to dream any dream, to become that dream bringing it forth to reality. I bought my best friend, Austin his tattoo as well. He got a cross tattoo, it was a great moment sharing that with him. It was his first tattoo, I haven't heard from Mariah for a few weeks. She called me up one day and told me we were having twins and sent me a pic of the ultrasound. I was very excited to know, I was having a girl too. We were going to name her, Kairi Paige. Mariah already had a daughter but her daughter was in state custody because her baby's daddy was on meth and Mariah lived in a children's home. She stopped seeing Chris. She left Chidhaven and moved in with her other baby's daddy. She got on meth and had a miscarriage killing my babies by doing drugs. I wrote these poems about that experience with her. This was a point in my life after finding out that information, I almost took my life. If it wasn't for Austin or God, I may have succeeded. I forgive everyone who has ever hurt me. Michael Jordan has a quote that I love I'm a good enough man to accept the good, but I'm a better man to accept the bad. Yo, I miss you, and I mean well but when I talked to you last, I shouldn't have yelled. See, I gave you my best, all the feelings were the real test. I wouldn't have fallen if I knew falling would land me in hell. Since you didn't fall through, I fell apart right before you…you made all the wrong moves which pushed me away into a new groove. I remember when we first met, you sat behind me in Mr. Metcalf's speech class. First time introducing myself, not even four hours later, you were hitting me up on the social media web, asking for a cell so you can call me on the dl. See, you were in a controlled environment, by choosing to play with mine and Chris's emotions trying to hide it, a beautiful hoe that wasn't the nicest! You were fighting to break free looking for freedom. I thought I was enough to set you free or was I actually trying to set me free? See, you stole my heart ripped it out and I laid there to bleed. Who is Chris? You see well, he's the guy that you would see when you weren't thinking of me. After a couple of months, speech class turned to mess. My heart was still dissected, pulled from my chest. I almost took my own life over some stupid bitch that would have been the death of T. T Harrison. Thank God for strength. Pulled me from the brink. The brink of despair, all my haters would have won see you won't take me out because I am a champion. See, God helped me out of that hell, opened my mind, and gave me the words to sell all of you. Now I'm chasing dreams, my shot groups are following through. These lyrics are flowing through me. I'm on autopilot, you goon. A professional in the field, my mind is a dictionary trapped in a cell. I hold the key, I'm freeing myself, get the hell out of my way or get the pen and pad I need help! Dreamer's code is a sentimental word, the name of my firstborn, you would have been two years old, but I lost you and your twin sister, Kairi Paige, it was all on your mother, she got lost in her age, when she took a hit you all were gone in a haze. That death pipe surely wasn't a phase. Possessed by a demon but it never freed her, after the first time she never feared her. Intoxicated by her love, she forgot about the tears of losing her twins after all the years, I wish you all were still here, but am I selfish for desiring that? For I know in time you all will appear. When this spirit leaves this body, it will be clear, we'll be in the same realm even after all these tears. We'll walk by the rivers together, I will always be near. For my Heavenly Father has a greater plan than I can comprehend. For when I pray I'm speaking in your ear. Thank you, Dad, for taking care of them, so grateful for this life, until we meet again. That isn't love when you're always getting hurt for when she tells you it's only you but she's out there, getting fucked. When she tells you that she loves you but she's out there doing drugs. For when you thought she saved your soul but she really ordered the hearse. So now you're on the run getting with all these hoes cause it's a lot of fun, drinking on this rum forgetting about your feelings because this girl pulled the gun. She killed the good you, now your sentence is done! Bulletproof another good soul that forgot how to tell the truth. You're making all this green cause you're on the move. Spilling the beans, it's how I tell the news. The girl that I used to love lost the best view, she disappeared, buried in my tears, she lost herself in her mind, so high that she got left behind. For I thought, my love would rekindle the fire, to save her soul while I was saving mine. It happened the other way though, it turned out to be a joke. For she lost herself in the pills, I lost myself in the smoke. For she never meant for me to get hurt, I knew what I was getting into, too much trust and belief really can hurt. So I'm letting go freeing my soul letting go of yesterday so I can grow. Forgiving her and forgiving my foes for the love that I gave away can never be sold. I found a different way, God released the hold, and the demons had on me fled, when I washed in the Holy Ghost. He led me to the show I'm no longer broke, setup every station to breathe life in these souls, the best relationship ever my Heavenly Father welcomes us home. The greatest of all love, what Jesus did for us at the cross! I think about you every day, is this love going to go away? See I put my heart on the line, put my love on the wire, now you're gone and I'm trying to rekindle the fire. Gone, you're gone away, out there with my love while I'm losing my way, taking this pain, getting dazed from the alcohol that has come to play. Gone but not forgotten you hold a place in my heart, it's a complex project. The memories we had don't seem to go away. When it's nighttime, I miss you and feel the same. If I could hold you in my arms, I'd hold you till I can't hold you anymore, carry you till my arms collapse as I fall to the floor. Love you till I can't love anymore, you got to the real me you broke through the door. When you got inside you saw, I'm not as perfect as you thought another broken soul that was traumatized by many thoughts. For the memories of my childhood always come to play a part. A hospital for the broken is what I need, a patient that needs to see a shrink. I am a poet that can dream any dream, or paint pictures with words about anything. Someone to love me even when I want to leave, someone that will hold me down for I'm scared they may leave so if it's me to leave first I won't have to experience the pain of them walking away, or leaving me out, standing in the rain. If I can keep the walls up, I will be okay but I will never be loved and that's not okay. I'm standing in your desert, can you see me? The wind is picking up, the dusty air, it's making it hard to breathe. I was wondering, if you could save me. If you would hold me down even when you're angry. Continue to take away the pain for I'll stay even if it's through the sad scenes. I'm writing all these papers since I left, of course, I had this pain in my head. Screaming and shouting from taking all this pain, I should have let you in, you were my medicine, God, why do I push away? When someone wants to love me, I want to run away. Afraid they may do the same as my mother did when I was in the 10th-grade, crying with the rain, I got to make a change. An emotional wreck, speaking to you, you can have the heart that's in my chest, I'm giving in, and I can't let you slip. I'll lose myself if I lose you. Don't want to be another memory that didn't come true. I don't know what it is but there's something about you, something so comforting it heals the cuts and bruises from when I was blue. This love has to be true because even through our faults, you give me all the clues. I've fallen for you, cutting the ropes, giving my all to you. Holding in you in my arms, I will never be that far, as long as you're thinking of me, I will be in your heart. Running my fingers through your hair, I will hold you when you're scared. This note I'm writing is for you. I need you, you reach me in ways like no one can. You haven't put in the grind like me you haven't put in the time like me you haven't lost your mind like me but you can if you only believe. I put my Lamborghini in drive and I'm cruising down the boulevard. I'm selling everything but drugs because I'm feeling like a pop star. If you want to be free like me then you better call up Kevin Hart. Life isn't what it seems, it so much more than the system that we were born into and blinded by. Everything physical was created by the spiritual. Earth and we humans are a reflection of God's kingdom. He created us out of his love, I'm so thankful that he thought of me when he planned creation; by choosing to place my soul in this human body. He created us to love and serve each other, as he has loved and served us; by giving us the opportunity to live this thing, called life. He's not distant and angry but is the complete expression of love. He loves us, he just wants us to develop a relationship with him. He didn't design it to be called religion either, just a relationship with our Heavenly Father. It satisfied God to crush Jesus that away our sins may be forgiven. So that we may be reconciled with God through Jesus Christ, our Lord! I see what they can't! I see the invisible! I want you all to know, I love you! You will grow through what you go through! God will reveal to you why he's taking you through the deep waters! Trust him. I'm a King, are you a King or a Queen? Are you doing what you have to do to become your best self to serve the world? I decided to break the basic cycle, it's a vicious circle! Become your BEST SELF! LIVE YOUR DREAM!

This is my passion and I'll take action. It's all about compassion, for your dreams. You can really be what you believe that's what's so incredible about being a human being. It's that we have something no other animal has. That is imagination, and what imagination allows us to do. It allows us to see it already happen in our mind before it takes place in reality.

You got off the elevator too early because I'm going up. I'm writing this because I'm no longer hurting. I gave my myself. She was a very sweet good girl, we dated for probably three months, I couldn't hold down the relationship. I was smoking weed every day. I couldn't survive a day without being high, I couldn't take on the sober reality of all of the pain I experienced. My car was having trouble starting in the mornings. I didn't realize it was just from the cold weather. Well, I was going to sell the car to Blake for $500. I trusted him so I let him hold onto the title too. I was working at McDonald's, around 40 hours a week, helping out with the rent and groceries. Blake and his mom started making fun of me every day. Being cruel with their words towards me, I dealt with it for two months. Before I started my job at McDonald's, we didn't have much food in the house, so I said a prayer.

I said, "God please forgive me for my sins, please help me God, we don't have much food to eat."

It wasn't even five minutes and $200 was added to my credit card line. I cried for God having mercy on me and blessing me with that miracle. It was around early July when I packed my bags, I only had $300. I didn't have enough money for gas to get my car across the states. I couldn't deal with Blake or Amber's negativity anymore so I parked my car brought my keys with me, caught a taxi to the bus station, called up Austin, he gave me the okay that I could come, stay with him at his house in New Baltimore, Michigan. I would have sold my car before I left but Blake hid the title and wouldn't give it to me. He said, he lost it and the funny thing is he wanted me to leave the keys with him. I would have to go all the way to the courthouse in Alabama to retrieve another title for the car so I let it go. I knew deep down there was something greater waiting for me but it was going to be rough for a while. It was such a relief when I boarded the bus. I was so thankful to be out of that toxic environment. The scenery was so beautiful as I traveled from the northwest to the northeast. I had met a girl on the bus that was from Australia meeting here is where I got the idea for the name, "Lucy" to use for this novel I am writing. The "I Couldn't Find Her So I Created Her" part of the title I got that phrase in my mind because I connected with a girl, named Kenzie on Tinder, we talked months six months but she was too shy to meet me. If it wasn't for her, I wouldn't have been inspired to write this novel or a lot of the poetry in it. She is a creative writing major and connecting with her really lit the fire in my heart, to write the most phenomenal work of art that was created. It took me three days of riding the bus to arrive at the Detroit bus station, Austin picked me up, we stopped at the store to buy some wraps and we lit up a blunt when we got to his house. He got me a job with him at elite fencing, it was great being with my best friend again on beautiful Lake St. Clair, Michigan is so breathtaking. After a month, I ended up moving into a hotel because Austin's girlfriend didn't like me being there, which pissed Austin off. I stayed in the hotel for two weeks. After doing hard labor for six weeks, I decided I was tired of running from the pain that I was going to go home and face the music. I had nowhere to go but my Dad's house sadly and I had been high every day for the past three years on weed. When I got to my dad's house was when I let go of the marijuana and stopped smoking. It was going to be six months till I started school. I was going to take one more semester of general courses then I was going to decide on a major. I fell into a deep dark depression being

This wasn't an epiphany moment, but it was the genesis of a realization that this could well be a career path for me! A week passed, and then I decided I'm going to develop this God given talent! I am so thankful I listened to my heart. I knew it wasn't going to be easy, but nothing worth developing comes easily! Nothing great comes from comfort zones and let me tell you every day spent in the Cosmetology program takes me out of my comfort zone! I am so grateful for that! God has brought me through so many storms and I realize now that if you give God control of your life, he will put you in control of your life! I am so blessed! The first week of school, I was very nervous, never in my life have I been surrounded by 50 or 60 women. It was really awkward for me. I didn't know exactly how to talk to girls. I was shy. I still dressed pretty fly though. My first four months in the program with Mrs. Moore were very challenging for me. I was moving my fingers in hands. I have never configured before, if I could describe in an analogy what it was like, it was as if I was crawling on my stomach in a maze trying to find my way out to get to the next level. Mrs. Moore was like the instructor from Mulan, somehow she was going to take us from default to make a stylist out of us. She wasn't mean at all she was strict but also very sweet and helpful. It didn't help either that Tannin was an overgrown bully always saying rude stuff to me after five to six weeks in the program. I messaged both of the teachers on Facebook and let them know what was going on. The next class day, they both sat me down in their office and questioned me on what tannin was saying to me. Afterward, they sat her down without me in there and talked to her. She gave me ugly looks that day and the next day but after that she never bothered me again.

In my 2nd semester, Mrs. Moore came up to me and said, "Tyler, you did really well on your tests last semester. We would love to have you on the Cosmetology Quiz Bowl team, to compete for the state championship at Skills USA."

I was like, "Yes, I will do it Mrs. Moore."

I studied for a good two to three months before we had our competition at the BJCC, and I was competing with four other competitors. They gave us a paper test, we had to turn in our resumes, then we had the quiz bowl competition, it was held privately in a room there at the BJCC.

I remember one question was, "Sally was using her curling iron, what measures the electricity of it?"

I pressed the button before they were finished saying the whole question. I said watt, everyone in the room busted out laughing, Jordan said Tyler they didn't finish asking the full question. I looked at them like what was going on because watt was the correct answer. They had thought I was asking 'what?' The judges laughed too and our team still got the point. We ended up winning the State Competition at Skills USA. I can still remember on awards day when they called us out as Gold Medalist, I had such a euphoric rush, it was so phenomenal, I couldn't believe that we did it. We walked up on stage, they all took our pictures, we each received our Gold Medal and our department got a banner for 2018 Cosmetology Quiz Bowl State Champions. We were winners because we are winners, it is our corps being, and that is why we are a success! I had just finished third semester this past summer, it was the last week of July of 2018 when I started on this novel, allowing you all to wonder inside my thoughts and imagination, and I hope you all enjoy the ride, I promise it isn't all dark, and that there is a light at the end of the tunnel. I got President's list twice in the program and Dean's list once. Next semester is my last semester till I have certificates in Salon and Spa Management with a license in Cosmetology. It takes courage to start again from nothing, but I am a champion and I always find a way that works. I love my classmates and my teachers, they are a true blessing in my life. It was during my first semester that I struggled the most with the hair program but I adapted well, it was also during this time I was sleeping in an RV in the cold it would get down to 20 degrees outside. I didn't have electricity or running water for four to five months straight. What pushed me to move into the RV was that my first week of school I came home like normal, put on a *Die Hard* movie with Bruce Willis, reclined in the recliner to enjoy the movie.

My dad came in the living room, he said, "Hey, Tyler, I got some coupons if you want to look through them."

I replied, "Yeah sure. I will look at them after I'm finished watching the movie."

He got in my face and said, "No, you're going to look at them right now."

I said, "I don't know, who you think you are but I am not your bitch, I am not your private so back the fuck off!"

He replied, "Get the fuck out."

So I packed all of my clothes and belongings in my duffel bag, and moved into the RV. Before I left the house when I was finished packing.

I ran around inside the house yelling at the top of my lungs, "You beat my brothers and my mom, you beat my brothers and my mom!" As he sat in his chair I told him "I'm going to let the world know who you really are."

I spent two hours, writing about my childhood and created a video. I titled it, Behind Closed Doors @xaldin254 and I posted it to YouTube. I held on despite of my circumstances and because of the iron will that I have. I will have certificates by December of 2018 in Salon and Spa Management with a license in Cosmetology. I am so grateful and blessed in spite of all of the tragedies I have experienced. I listen to speeches by Les Brown, Jim Rohn, Eric Thomas, Tony Robbins, Tom Bilyeu, Gary Vee, Inky Johnson, and many more motivational coaches every day, because we are all buying someone's plan, the question is who has you talked into doing what you're doing? If I could describe what it is like to love someone you have never met, I would tell you it is like loving that person for your entire life. This is my story Lucy, this was my blueprint till up to this point, and I have been working to shift that to create a whole new sketch.

She gasped, "Whoa that was a lot. It was if I was watching a movie of you as you were telling me your life story."

I gave her some tissue because she was weeping. She wanted me to take her back to her place. "Tyler, I will contact you in a few days, it's going to take a few days for me to digest all of that information you shared with me."

I pulled into her driveway, got out of the car to open her door, I hugged her. "I really enjoyed tonight, you were the first one to hear all of my stories, and I am blessed to be able to share my life with someone that truly understands me."

As I drove off she looked at me in the most inspiring way. I was headed to the beach tonight, there isn't anything like walking on the white sand, as the water breaks at the shore, as my life opens up, I open the last door, that I have held shut for so long, I don't feel the pain anymore, not the best at painting pictures but I can with writing on paper, words are my paint, this pen is the brush, I can open any mind while hushing any fuss, for this gift is woven in me it is very lush, I can hear the seagulls call, I wonder what they are thinking, I wonder what it is like, to not hear anything at all. To see the physical anyone can do but to sense the dynamics of someone who was abused takes someone special, someone who can see past the room. Someone who can see the spirit in someone flutter, for the ashes and dust, don't rust the spirit, the body they can touch but the spirit they can't crush. What is love, what is beauty? What is this rush that is so consuming? What is the meaning of life? What is the meaning of this movement? For I am overflowing with love, overflowing with beauty, I'm chasing every lost soul out there to bring life to your tune, you can be anything you want that is what's so moving! The lights of the restaurant on the beach light up, I walk up to it, I am pretty hungry considering I haven't ate anything. I pulled up to take a seat. I ordered a large sweet tea to drink with shrimp scampi as my entree. There was a guy covered in tattoos sitting in the corner, he looked very familiar.

"Austin, what is up my brother how have you been? You never told me, you were coming down to Panama City."

"Yeah brother, I knew you were in this area, Molly and I broke up, what a better way to end the relationship than to drive down to Panama City to surprise my best friend."

"What? Has it been three years since I have seen you?"

We both ordered a beer to celebrate.

"Hey, Austin, I hear of talks of hidden treasure in one of these caverns on this island. Are you up for an adventure brother?"

"With you hell yeah man, modern day treasure hunters, you must be living life Tyler."

"I am man living life to the fullest, hey Austin before we start our treasure exploration lets go skydiving tomorrow!"

"Skydiving, what are you nuts, Tyler? I am not jumping from a perfectly good airplane."

With a little bit of persuasion, Austin was down for the jump. The next day was here.

Lucy messaged me, "Good morning, handsome, how are you? I know I said a couple of days but can we get together for dinner tonight at Red Lobster?"

I replied, "Sure, I would love to. I'm about to jump out of an airplane so if I have a safe landing, I will see you tonight."

She replied, "Okay I will see you at five."

I called up Preston, my little brother, to come jump with us as well. We all met at ten in the morning, when we got there we had to sign waivers, we had to each pay $200 to go skydiving. We watch a video on Tandem Skydiving, suit up with the guys we are jumping with, then we boarded the plane. We flew up to 14,000 feet in the air, the jumpers told us that we may forget how to breathe when we jump so in order to breathe you got to scream. They were right you did have to scream in order to breathe, I wasn't scared of jumping, and I was more excited and pumped! Austin was afraid, I went first so he would see that I wasn't going to back out! Once you don't fear death anymore what is there left to fear? As I flew through the air it felt like my brain was melting. It was such an incredible rush, such a euphoric rush it was mind blowing, all my fears melted in the way in the face of death it was such a blissful experience. I lifted my legs up as I came in for the landing. My skydiver's name was Owen Greer, he was a cool dude.

"Austin what did you think of that?"

"Bro, I think I'm going to be sick."

There he goes throwing up.

"Well gentleman, it was a pleasure jumping with you all, thank you for skydiving with Skydive Panama."

They request Owen next time to come. We had purchased the video too so Austin, Preston and I both had a cameraman jump with us as well so we got the footage. I definitely was going to put our footage on YouTube. Austin and I went to get some Mexican food for lunch.

"Bro that was so awesome! Thank you for coming with me to skydive, I am glad we got to experience that! I am feeling like a million dollars."

My perceptions and views on life were shifted. I now saw life in this heavenly divine way that was so magical how we are such incredible creatures. I love some chips and salsa with grilled chicken and cheese quesadilla stuffed with grilled bell pepper. Man, that is my favorite meal to eat. We shuffle and hustle making a little bit of a bustle we paid for our lunch now it was time to go work our muscles. We were hitting up the gym, we may even take a little swim, run up the stairs, I'm looking for my twin, maybe he can give me the leads and tell me how to win, teach me how to grin, show me the ropes, give me some medicine, I came here to represent, I came here to let them in, if you say you're about it then you better settle in, this is T Hair and I'm coming live dancing on this stage as I'm preaching to you about life, this is what I see, this is what I do, I be hopping around the world like I'm a kangaroo, running up this money you can call me a monsoon because when I roll through town I'm always on the move! I am a writer and poet a singer and a showman, planted my seeds at the bottom they finally started growing, even when I was at my low end I planted my seeds in the dirt you best believe they started growing. See you can have anything you want in life, you can have anything you want even if you don't feel alright. I will pull on you all like a thief in the night because y'all don't know I'm here and that is alright. See I am the one I am the greatest I'm impacting you all for that is what my name represents. T Harrison in the flesh, never second-guessing the test for the power of God is woven in my chest I love my savior Jesus Christ he appointed me to be the best. I can write about anything I will love you even if you are mean for our nature calls us to love everything and these demons roaming around want to keep you from planting your seeds, would you give him your life? For he gave you this life, would you follow your dreams? Instead of being blinded by the blind man who wants to cut off your wings. See in the land of the blind the one-eyed man is king, even though these people have two eyes can they really see? For I have only one I and they will not put the blindfold on me. I am running to the top, I'm gaining momentum with every word that I drop, I'm searching for the one who will listen to me, open their ears to a young man who can see anything for I am a visionary it is how I write these things I can see the invisible it's because I still have my wings. The system says grow up, get a job that you don't care for, be slave nine to five, live paycheck to paycheck, being a slave to reality. See your personality becomes your personal reality, we all have a choice, follow your dreams or follow someone else's. I wish they would have taught me in school that it is okay not to be good at algebra for everyone's talent lies in something, for I didn't graduate high school but I did college. I jumped through the math hoop just so I could swim in the stream I wanted to swim in. I jumped through the class to look at me now, I'm still winning. Austin and I jumped on the elliptical, we ran for a good 40 minutes, then we lifted weights, see when you fall down it always give you the opportunity to get back up and grow stronger. We would bring our bodies to muscle failure so we would grow stronger, strong mind, strong spirit, and a strong body. The trinity of being strong, we are designed to be physically, mentally, and spiritually in shape. After our workout, we rinsed off then got in the hot tub. Whoa, there is nothing greater than working out hard then relaxing in the hot tub when finished. It was around 4:00 p.m. now too so it was time for us to get ready to go, Austin went back to his place while I got ready for my date with Lucy. I drove a 2018 Dodge Hellcat, over 700 horsepower it had it was green with black stripes, talk about a sporty car it was magnificent it would roar, I got dressed, put my Hellcat in the drive, and headed to Lucy's house. She was wearing an oxford blue colored romper with pink flowers on it. She took my breath away as I pulled into her driveway my jaw dropped and I gasped for air. I got out of the car to open her door, when her eyes caught mine it was if I was seeing her for the first time, lost in the momentum she was finding me by each second where her spirit connect with mine as we stared into each other's eyes. If someone was to say magic isn't real I would say they aren't a believer. For whatever you believe you will see and if not yet in the physical you will see it in the invisible. Brown hair, brown eyes with a smile so sweet she could pass as a dessert. The twinkle in her eyes gave me a feeling that I couldn't disguise for she was the one, she was going to save my life. "It is great to see you, Lucy. How are you?"

"I am doing great. I missed you and I have really thought about you. It was very unique how you opened up to me last night. I figured since you did that, I will open to you over dinner tonight."

"I can't wait to hear about you and learn more about you, Lucy."

"Sounds great!"

We arrived at Red Lobster, our hostess sat us down, and the scent of cheese biscuits fill the air, the aroma was so astounding I could taste them in my mouth. I was so pumped for a delicious dinner and to hear Lucy's story, I pulled her chair back as she sat down.

"Tyler, I am non-binary."

"What does that mean?"

"Well, I was born female-bodied but I have traits from male and female because of my chromosome make-up. The term 'non-binary' can mean different things to different people. At its core, it's used to describe someone whose gender identity isn't exclusively male or female. If someone tells you, they're non-binary, it's always important to ask what being non-binary means to them. Some people who are non-binary, experience their gender as both male and female, and others experience their gender as neither male nor female. Non-binary can also be used as an umbrella term, encompassing many gender identities that don't fit into the male-female binary. Although non-binary is often regarded as a new idea, the identifier has been around for as long as civilization has. In fact, non-binary gender has been recorded as far back as 400 B.C. to 200 A.D., when Hijras – people in India who identified as beyond male or female – were referenced in ancient Hindu texts. India is one of many countries around the world with language and a social culture that acknowledges those whose gender can't be exclusively categorized as male or female. I also have Turner's syndrome which has to do with me being non-binary."

"Wow! That is very interesting. I am extremely fascinated. What it Turner's syndrome to be exact?"

"Turner syndrome is a chromosomal condition that affects development in females. The most common feature of Turner syndrome is short stature, which becomes evident by about age five. An early loss of ovarian function (ovarian hypo function or premature ovarian failure) is also very common. The ovaries develop normally at first, but egg cells (oocytes) usually die prematurely and most ovarian tissue degenerates before birth. Many affected girls do not undergo puberty unless they receive hormone therapy, and most are unable to conceive (infertile). A small percentage of females with Turner syndrome retain normal ovarian function through young adulthood. About 30 percent of females with Turner syndrome have extra folds of skin on the neck (webbed neck), a low hairline at the back of the neck, puffiness or swelling (lymphedema) of the hands and feet, skeletal abnormalities, or kidney problems. One-third to one-half of individuals with Turner syndrome are born with a heart defect, such as a narrowing of the large artery leaving the heart (coarctation of the aorta) or abnormalities of the valve that connects the aorta with the heart (the aortic valve). Complications associated with these heart defects can be life threatening. Most girls and women with Turner syndrome have normal intelligence. Developmental delays, nonverbal learning disabilities, and behavioral problems are possible, although these characteristics vary among affected individuals. Turner syndrome is related to the X chromosome, which is one of the two sex chromosomes. People typically have two sex chromosomes in each cell: females have two X chromosomes, while males have one X chromosome and one Y chromosome. Turner syndrome results when one normal X chromosome is present in a female's cells and the other sex chromosome is missing or structurally altered. The missing genetic material affects development before and after birth. About half of individuals with Turner syndrome have monosomy X, which means each cell in the individual's body has only one copy of the X chromosome instead of the usual two sex chromosomes. Turner syndrome can also occur if one of the sex chromosomes is partially missing or rearranged rather than completely absent. Some women with Turner syndrome have a chromosomal change in only some of their cells, which is known as mosaicism. Women with Turner syndrome caused by X chromosome mosaicism are said to have mosaic Turner syndrome. Researchers have not determined which genes on the X chromosome are associated with most of the features of Turner syndrome. They have, however, identified one gene called *SHOX* that is important for bone development and growth. The loss of one copy of this gene likely causes short stature and skeletal abnormalities in women with Turner syndrome[3].

I was diagnosed at five years old, my plan was to never tell anyone to keep it a secret my whole life. I feel like it will be beneficial to people if I make a video about it and it may help people feel less alone that are dealing with the same stuff that I am or similar things. So when I was five, I was diagnosed with Turner's syndrome, what that means is that I have a piece of my 2nd X chromosome missing. Girls have two X chromosomes and girls with Turner's can have one X chromosome or can have a piece of their 2nd X chromosome missing. I'm going to tell you about my childhood and how it was growing up with Turner's. So what that meant for me is starting at age five, I had to start taking growth hormone shots every night, and I didn't stop taking growth hormone shots until I was 15, the reason I had to take shots was because girls with Turners have short stature because we don't make enough growth hormone to grow normally on our own. We grow but we just don't make enough growth hormone, I would be like 4'6" or 4'7". I am only 5'1" now, so I would be much, much shorter if I hadn't

---

[3] https://ghr.nlm.nih.gov/condition/turner-syndrome#genes.

had those shots every night. I just remember being a little kid and being terrified that my extended family like my grandma, my aunt and my grandpa would find out I was a freak that had to take shots to grow. That terrified me. I didn't want anybody knowing, let alone my friends in elementary school. The self-hatred started in probably late elementary school, I resented everything about me that was different, every single thing about me that was different. I resented the fact that I wasn't normal and you know what is even normal really? It was a dumb thing to think but that was my thought process as an eight and nine year old. Puberty was an entirely different story and things got even worse because girls with Turner's don't make enough estrogen on their own to go through puberty at a normal rate. So about age 11 or 12, I had to start taking extra hormones. I had to take estrogen supplements, to go through puberty normally. I started comparing my body to other girls and it was pretty much torture because I knew in my head that I was not going to move through puberty as fast as a lot of other people. I beat myself up over it because I hated the fact that I was skinny, I hated that my boobs weren't as big as other people. I recently learned the fact that when you're going through puberty and you learn the fact that you may never have biological kids, you start resenting your body basically. I am sorry that I am taking a while to get this entire out."

"Oh no, you are fine, Lucy. Keep on going, I am listening."

"See, you start resenting your body and you don't feel very womanly, I didn't feel like I fit in with girls and I didn't feel like I fit in with guys either. I was stuck in this gray in-between place and I didn't know about the term intersex because I had never been on Tumblr before. I know people make fun of Tumblr because it is so social justice but I love social justice! So I will proudly be a social justice warrior and I am not ashamed to be a Tumblr kid but I hadn't researched on the internet before because I just didn't want to think about having a genetic disorder. I didn't want to have to think about myself not being normal and I even in just the last year or so I have become really comfortable calling myself intersex. I am comfortable saying that I don't fit inside the binary of gender, I feel like there is so much more than girl or boy, you know what I mean? Yes, I do Lucy I understand you completely. See you look at the transgender community and you this beautiful array of different gender expressions. They are not ashamed, it makes me feel so free to see drag queens and stuff like that, get up on stage and put on makeup. Not that you had to put on makeup to find yourself or be yourself but it's just there are so many bold statements out there that show us that gender isn't binary. Yet you have YouTubers, making videos on how there are only two genders. I am living proof that there are not just two genders I am proud to call myself intersex. I am proud to call myself non-binary because it just so happens, I don't fit into the definitions of girl or boy. I am comfortable being in that middle ground, between both and I have fought this for years, I have fought for years to feel womanly and you know that never really happened and why do I have to try to feel womanly? Just so I can fit inside the box of a girl just because of my chromosomes. I actually I enjoy not being normal, I am finally at the point in my life where I am glad I am not like everybody else. Actually this

Friday I am going for some testing, to find out whether or not I will be able to have biological kids. I will never be able to conceive naturally, obviously because of my genetic disorder, but they aren't sure if I have viable eggs that they could possibly use for in vitro fertilization. The doctors did a few tests when I was younger and thought that I didn't know I found out that they didn't do all of the full testing that they should have. So I am going to find out Friday whether or not I will be able to freeze my eggs to have future kids, and that is a really big and scary thing for me. I have also made peace with the fact that I can't wait to adopt kids one day with whomever I marry, a girl or a boy or a non-binary or a Tran's person. I am just finally happy and okay with myself and that took nearly 20 years. If anybody else with genetic disorders or anybody else that is transgender that doesn't fit into the binary or society's definition of normal. You are okay, there is nothing wrong with you I promise and as much as your mind wants to tell you that there is something wrong with you there is not. You are beautiful and amazing just as you are and uhh, tears are falling, I am sorry. I believe the universe makes everything happen for a reason, I know that sounds really cliché but I believe that because all of my life, I have fought so hard to be normal and I finally realize that maybe I am meant for more. Maybe if all of us were this cookie-cutter idea of humans then life wouldn't be as beautiful. I am happy to say I am intersex, pansexual, non-binary, and you can call me a special snowflake all you want and I am sorry for crying. I just have never really talked about all of this that much 'sniffles' but you can call me a special snowflake all you want but I believe I was made the way I was for a reason. I am finally learning to appreciate that and I hope that sharing my story can help you guys learn to appreciate yourselves as well. I am going to stop before I turn into a crying mess but I love you guys and I want to be here for you guys that have trouble fitting in. It is okay to stand out and be different from the world. I love you guys. Hopefully, I can educate you all on this topic in a clear impacting way. A lot of people don't know about the intersex disorder, they don't know about genetic disorders, they don't know about people that biologically fall out of the binary. The gender binary because biological sex isn't even concrete, ha-ha, because you can have so many variations of genes. Anyways I was going to tell you guys I found out I will never be able to have biological kids after the testing. I got the results from the doctors and I found out in concrete that I wouldn't be able to. I had a feeling, I would never be able to because when I was 12 and 13, they did some blood tests. There is a certain hormone, Estradiol that indicates fertility and my blood did not come back with very much of that hormone in it. So the doctors told me ten years ago nearly that I didn't have much of a chance that I would have biological kids. So I was prepared for that, recently like I was saying my endocrinologist said I could have eggs and there's a chance that he could freeze them. I could have in vitro fertilization later on, so that gave me so much hope I was literally so nervous when I went to the doctor. I was just like my entire life could change, so I went in and I had a transvaginal ultrasound, which is as horrible as you could think it sounds ha-ha. It is a very invasive procedure and I hope none of you guys have to have it done hopefully ha-ha. It turned out, I only have the right half of my ovary. It is not very developed, there is an egg-like material on the ovary but they aren't viable. So I found out I can't have kids so I am going to have to adopt, while I have had years to kind of know this was probably coming my way. That this was going to be a wrench thrown into my plans because I have always wanted to be a parent, ever since I was little. It has been one of my biggest dreams is to be a parent, I use to play with dolls, I use to have tea parties with dolls, I use to have little doll beds that I would put them to bed in. I had always had that instinct that I wanted to be a parent, but I guess with the strongest appeal of having a biological kid is that it is half you and half of the other person that you love. So it just, it's very kind of devastating to know that I will never have a kid that is half me and half the person I love. It also does a lot to your self-confidence because my biological sex is female. Well, I identify as intersex now because I don't think female is accurate because my chromosomes are not matching to female. I was raised female, female is on my birth certificate it just is always a thing. You grow up and people will be like oh you're going to be a great mother one day, you're going to find a great guy, you're going to have kids. You're going to get pregnant and you're going to have this wonderful life and then in an instant because of a genetic disorder that entire dream, I am sorry for stuttering so much. That entire dream is shattered for me so it is very hard to cope with, um, and also when you get in your early 20s, there are some kids that I have gone to high school with that are already having two and three kids of their own already. When you can't have kids and when you are infertile you just feel like something is wrong with you. You feel as if you are falling behind, I know a lot of kids in their 20s feel like they are falling behind because they haven't met the right person yet. They don't know when they are going to have kids but they still know it is in their future, they still know it can actually happen. If they find the right person, but for me, it's just that is never going to happen, that is something I have to cope with. As I have gotten older, I kind of have seen the universe piece things together because I started exploring my gender identity more and feeling more comfortable calling myself intersex and non-binary. I am more comfortable being in that gray area, I don't have to be, I don't have to conform to male or female, I can just be feminine and I can be masculine, I can just be Lucy. I was talking to one of my friends about it a month or two ago, she was like, if you had been able to have kids, if you were able to get pregnant would that give you really bad gender dysphoria and I was like yeah ha-ha it probably would. So it is almost a blessing in disguise that I won't have to go through pregnancy not that I wouldn't ever want to but it probably would be very difficult for someone of my gender identity to go through that. I believe everything happens for a reason and I believe that one day I am supposed to adopt a wonderful child that doesn't have a home. I am going to give them a great home, and I am going to be a great parent one day. So I am looking forward to that, and I hope I find the right person to be a parent with. I am happy being a 21-year-old person having fun and living my life being creative and not worrying about things. But yeah it still is I wanted to let you know that I can't have kids because I feel like you should know. I love people so much life is such a beautiful creation. I may not be able to have kids but I can create with the gifts that God did give me so I can share and impact millions of people in the universe."

"Whoa, that is incredible, I am at loss for words, Lucy. You are something so more than I imagined…I support you in every way based on your beliefs and values. I really am fond of you, the way you compose thoughts and ideas. We should create an organization that represents love for everyone that reaches out to cause an uprise, a movement that reaches out and rescues people from the system we are blinded by. An organization that reaches out and rescues damaged human beings providing a safe haven for them to prosper in. We will provide classes on loving ourselves, classes on loving others, and classes on loving our God. For who am I to judge anyone when I have black sin on my hands too, we were put here to love and serve each other. We will also hold classes that will help people identify with the truest version of themselves so that they can develop themselves to become the greatest version of themselves. I know it sounds like a lot of work, it is a lot of work but step by step we will move closer and closer to our goal. Providing shelter and food to be able to make this happen, I will write a novel telling about your life and my life, and half of the proceeds that we make from selling the novel we will use to fund the organization. We will name it, Choose Love Not Hate, what do you think Lucy?"

"I love it, gosh you have such an inspiring way about you despite the things you have been through you still look for the good in life, and you still find happiness despite how many times the world took it from you. I find you as a role model, you are helping me find happiness while this is just our 2nd date, and I have never had a connection with someone like this before. You really amaze me, Tyler. I am grateful to you!"

"So what college did you go to, Lucy?"

"Funny you should ask. Well I wrote down a list of five different destinations for myself. My 1st choice was to go to Julliard, NYU, or Columbia and audition for lots of Broadway stuff. My 2nd choice was to go to Yale to become a doctor. My 3rd choice was to go to Brown University and become a writer becoming anything I wanted. My 4th choice was to go to NYU and become a drama major. My 5th choice was to go to Oxford and become a lawyer. I grew up in Nashville, TN. I ended up going to the University of Chattanooga for film editing, and directing. I love to creative write as well, I write in my journal every day of different things I experience, from emotions to places, or certain people I interact with that day. I believe that with writing we can unlock a lot of our dreams and desires because we are giving someone else the opportunity to admire how magical the cave is inside of our minds. It truly is a gift from God our minds are, we can create an emotion by creating a thought or change an emotion by changing our thoughts. Have you ever wondered what it would be like if we all wrote a story about our lives? The people we could change by changing ourselves, we could shift their personal philosophy by sharing our personal philosophy with them. It is such an amazing world, such an elegantly beautiful planet that we get to roam about on."

"You draw me in with your intellectual mind, it opens my eyes allowing me to see more with my sight, I move along outside while walking next to you by your side, you fascinate me, the more that you open your mind, you change me by letting me see past your disguise for we both are raw and truthful that is how the chemistry flies when we are leading our own lives. I could run, jump, scream, and sigh but I can't get you off my mind. I could journey through the day, pretending that I'm fine, but even you know the truth…When I'm without you, I'm not alright…You have the prettiest blue eyes, they are blue just like the sky and when you are walking by I am possessed by the twinkling of your eyes…If you weren't so shy I would fall asleep in your arms every night, if it was up to me you would be mine, I can't seem to let you go for without you I'm a carving in a stone, a story that only you can complete for we were made to grow old. I could tell you that I love you but those words have an empty ring but I could show you that I love you by letting you deep inside of my dreams. For Lucy, you are an angel, you are not a scheme, you are more than what they perceive, and you are my diamond ring."

"Whoa, Tyler, that was phenomenal, you are really good with your poems, do you happen to have a copy?"

"Yes I do, I have a copy of some poems I have written in the car, I will pay for dinner, walk you out to my car then retrieve the documents."

It was such a beautiful night clear skies with the moon so vividly bright, I looked Lucy in her eyes, leaned in and kissed her cheek, I hugged her and paused, for these two new loves were starting to fall. I opened the car door while she got in, I walked around to my side got in and drove her to her house. When I pulled into her driveway, I put it the car in park, she leaned in and kissed me on the lips, this was our first kiss.

"I really enjoyed tonight, thank you for all that you do. Would you like to come in and spend the rest of the night with me? I would like to read through your poems, Tyler."

"I would love to stay over with you, Lucy."

We got inside. I sat down on her couch with her and she began reading some of my poems. Hey, Kenz, I got some cool friends, yes I am a Gemini you can call me twins, I know you just met me, you don't have to play pretend, that I got your heart in the palm of my hands, I think about you from time to time, wonder if you wonder, what I'm doing with mine, I am oh so thankful your apart of my life, never would have thought, you and I would be intertwined, from connecting on a dating app we started online, who knows where this road will go, but that's okay we will be just fine, it's oh so cool how I can rhyme in this rhyme, about this beautiful girl I just met who is oh so kind, you can be my queen, I'll never let your crown fall, can't wait to hear you sing, we'll ride horses by the sea, travel the waters from sea to shining sea, were both on the journey to getting college degrees, to develop ourselves, to grow our wings. I don't know if you know this, but I been searching for you in my dreams, I've prayed many times got down on my knees God send me a woman to rescue me, to talk to and hold, to watch her be bold, to go on adventures with, to the store, to go to church with, to praise the Lord, to share my life with and all my goals, to hold her close I'll even wash her clothes maybe this poem I wrote won't have her tripping on her tippy toes.

Say something or I'm giving up. I need you to speak. I'm placing my trust in you if you want to leave then it's up to you but I'm begging you darling, I'd cry in your arms. I've got everything to lose. So let's just have dinner for two let's talk this over, believe in the new. For when I'm with you the skies aren't so blue you changed me and all that I do.

So let's go for a walk in the park, no social media just your heart and my heart lay down on the grass admire your art the beauty of your eyes lights up the dark hold your hand you hold mine for you and I are a fragment of time so let's not fuss or fight lets love each other until the end of our lives. I'll love your soul if you love mine, I'll be your man, and you'll be my wife. Let's travel this land, build sand castles in the sand, watching the high tide go. I'll walk the beaches with you even when we're old. Awed by how beautifully we've grown, and how this love started 40 years ago. Valentines is tomorrow so you should know that I will love you as our life unfolds, chase your dream and I'll chase mine for when you get home you'll still be mine! Happy Valentine's Day!

Roses are beautiful, they do have thorns but I don't fear reaching to pick one for there is always a possibility I may get pricked but if I don't reach out to grab one, I may never know the beauty and love of holding one without the pain.

We'll be kissing and loving like we are some kangaroos. See I can love you how I want because I'm Winnie the pooh, you can hold me like you want because you got the moves and I'll be moving along in sync with your grooves.

So as I lay here in the dark, I can see the real you. I can see your heart. Breathing slowly, eyes are closing, listening to your heartbeat while you are asleep. Where are you in your dreams? Searching for the real thing, searching for the real me, your soul is protected, standing guard of your temple. We're finally free, so come along with me, in the beginning, it can be scary, but tell me would you be there if I couldn't see? If I couldn't read, but I could hear your beautiful voice sing. Searching for the real thing, searching for my queen, I'm no longer hurting. If you get close to me, please be patient, 'cause I been broken. It's how I'm built and it's urgent, I am flowing, damn, I am growing, damn I am sewing, damn I am onto things that I couldn't believe. You are my only, would you ride with me? Would you hide with me? Would you stand side by side with me? Stand by me, equipping you with my dreams. Dreaming with my eyes open its how I see. Now hold up take a minute. Composing this only took me ten minutes. Writing about my woman I am the lion she's not the culprit, she is my lover, she is. We are going to make it past every test. Acing them now it's time to rest. Tucking in my girl, I found the world while I'm in the world, laying my head on her lap, joining her while she takes a nap. First, let me take a snap of my beauty drooling. Silly cute things, she'll see it in the morning. Goodnight all you listeners.

I miss you and it's hard to sleep, as I lay here in bed I find it hard to breathe…For when I'm without you my life is incomplete…I need to journey with your spirit to help unlock me, come lay down with me, as I stare into your eyes I can feel you breathe, the way your heart beats is a rhythm that screams, love from inside your chest, can you hear the wind blow? For the way, it shakes our mind, when the temperature is low, it has me yearning for your presence to fight off the cold. Kiss me with your lips, rescue me with your grip, and please be true to me for my walls are very thin. I'm searching for a lifelong friend, a companion that doesn't play pretend, will this love last? Or will it pass us by leaving us on our ass? For you fight for me when my hands are tired, you pick up the slack I'm grateful for that. Sorry for being so tough on you…I just want us to last…To make it through…Relationships today what can I say they are like a joke. I promise I'm done with the childish games, for when I found you my life and values changed…I want you to be mine always every day 🔒

What if I told you I didn't feel good and I'm broken? What if I told you I'm falling out, been struggling loving. See it's lonely at the top, that's something I learned and even though I'm alone, I still have purpose, I just happened to think, maybe you were worth it, so I spent time chasing, trying to cope, losing myself in my shame, but I don't feel deserted for they always leave and I'm always hurting. Lonely at the top, but you do eat great, I may not have someone to love but why should I complain, I chose this way bout to warm up this ribeye steak, with a glass of Moscato with my plate. Hate cannot drive out hate, love can only do that, serve and love is the only way to be great. I'm good at being a player for I been playing games since I was eight, but I'd give up these childish games for the right lady. I am going up, watch me work, I'm blowing up. I'm searching for some love, fighting for some love, you can even call me Herc. I'm running out of love since Mariah left. I started going numb, please help me, and hurry up. Wanted to heal your scars, I end being scarred. In life, it can be hard. See you can have me but you can't have my heart because it's fragile and I may fall apart if someone hurts me again. All it will take is one more scar.

So you're called Mickey? Mickey Mouse? Let's party in your clubhouse, happy vibes never going to shut it down, with Donald and Goofy riding around, watch when they try to hide, let me find where they at, smoking up our loud, got a college degree, we made our parents proud, were floating on the cloud, eyes are red as hell, mickey mouse clubhouse, never shut it down, welcoming every crowd! Yes, we're on the news, yes, we're making moves, yes, we're paper view, yes, we're changing views, yes were overdue, moving up, blew up, way too soon, listen, please stay attuned...I'm from a different crew, I make boss moves, got the best sauce too! I had to get new shoes, I learned in school, never lets these fools mock you, walking to my car, headed to the bar, open up the door, what are you waiting for, hop up in my ride, yes were getting high, I hope you don't mind, I am about that life, yes I'm representing light, yes I'm speaking right, pedal to the metal, no heavy metal, setting a new schedule, every time I hit, I'm raw, found me a fine job, rapping on the sidewalk, with my bandana dog. Grew up in a trailer park, it's where I learned how to spark, speaking words with my heart, writing is a phenomenal art. I grew up in the dark, I had a come apart, there's light in my heart. I jumped off the porch, watch how I torch, I won't be ignored, I've dated a few girls, they turned out to be whores, I'm searching for the one, please let me find her Lord. I will carry the torch, I'm making police reports, these niggas phony watch your cards, these niggas phony watch your cars, gold on my lawn, I'm gassing up my spaceship dog, shopping at every mall, yes I'm fresh as hell, these niggas are close, be aware. I had to walk through hell, that's how I paid my bail, that's how I beat the jail, got freedom, fresh as hell, and got my freedom fresh as hell! Lost in my passion, speaking is my action, breathing is for traction, I'm looking for her in my mansion, yes she likes dirty dancing, I am her companion, she has compassion.

Maybe I took it too fast while we were taking it slow, I tried to slow down, but my brakes are broke. When I get in my feelings I get scared and alone, afraid you won't catch me when I fall. I'll know better next time though, it's okay to listen to your heart but don't lose control, when things get shaky and out of control, take a step back remember your only 21 years old. Yes, it does get a little cold when you're left with nothing just the memories that can be told. I know I'm still young, but I want to be in love, to share my life with this free spirit soul. Here lately things have been distant, I pray you're not letting go, or letting him in, for I wanted you to be my best friend, and for you to tell me all about John Lennon. I know he is a music man, I can't wait to learn about what he represents. Or where this road is taking us because to me you're Heaven Sent,

I blame it on my ADHD, it's God's gift to me, hyperactivity it's how I breathe, no I do not do speed, this gift is woven in me. Naturally high, it's how I fly, Ty Guy if it isn't fly, it isn't right. If you don't grind you won't reach the gold mine. Pouring a glass of wine, Welcome to the party, work hard, play hard, then you'll be alright. Waking up early, it's time to shine, a typical day in the office, rolling up this green, operating from dream to dream. I am searching for my queen. I only need one girl, she is my beauty. We both be shooting scenes, behind the scenes, producing is our niche, it's our click, we're making movies, let's rewind time for a minute. I remember when we first met. It all started on the internet. Social media isn't as evil as they make it, for I found my queen while marketing.

Baby you're my everything, the search is over I believe, for I'll be your king. I love the attention you give me, for it's deeper than the fake love I use to get, I was lonely till I found my Honey, I believe in her and she believes in me. We are changing states, escaping fakes, she is my peace, she is great. I look forward to every week I get to spend with her, being goofy, even when she's moody, she the best view and most important. Unheard words, nothing comes close, to these verses, of this boy and girl who found each other on earth. I been getting it out the dirt, turned my F's to A's, I killed the old me, he was standing in my way. Listen, baby, you will never hurt unless it's just my time to go. For when God calls me home and I leave this Earth, just know I'm still with you and you're still in my heart, don't know if I'll get tomorrow, so I'm telling you today, leading the way. Let's take this moment in, let our hearts blend, live in the present, one day at a time, that's a lot of presents. It's what I represent. 🎵🎵

So I met this girl today, her name was Haylee, knew from the jump she was a little crazy, didn't stop me from wanting to date. She thought, she could play me, ha-ha it's okay, she set up my Plan B. Her name was Harley, it was her bestie. I stuck to Haylee till she started faking, so I was onto the Plan B, onto the Plan B, onto the Plan B, started seeing Harley, went to the cheesecake factory, and had a little party! Caught a case of the feelings, oh shit dog can you believe this?! Shit is crazy, I don't catch feelings, what am I feeling? Now this girl is playing me, she got me in sync, distracting me from my dreams…I'm just trying to make green, cruising in my limousine, girl I got everything, wanted you on my team, till you started faking. Knew you

73

were playing, knew you were playing and knew you were playing me...Oh shit what happened to my Plan B, you were my lady, plain out shady. Girl, you don't phase me, Girl, you don't phase me, Girl, you don't phase me. I would have given everything for you my time, energy, and love now I'm getting crunk. Whipping my big truck, there will never be us. Stood me up lost trust, stood me up lost trust, stood me up lost trust, tried to corrupt, tried to corrupt. That hurt you did knock me down, I will always stand ground, I will always stand proud. Rising up to the Crowd, yes you know I'm blowing loud. Can you hear my shout? Got energy in this rap, I got all kinds of hats, spitting raw, that is how I trap. Yes, I live underground, speaking life into every town. On the journey, on-demand Harley, I would have been your man. Represent the seconds we spent, letting this out is healing. Forgiveness is key, I forgive you all for playing me. I'm onto Plan C, Cosmetology. Racking up this degree, doing hair sets me free, I believe in make-believe. Love your boy T. You got off the elevator too early cause I'm going up. The reason I'm writing this I'm no longer hurting. I just find this experience funny. I gave you my heart but you couldn't hold it. I got it back now it is back to learning!

So let me tell you a story about the circulatory no it's not boring so don't let me catch you snoring! This is not a warning, you better believe, I'm making this speech in the morning. Learning and swerving spreading our wings time to get soaring. Found the keys to success, everything I live for I'm here to confess. T Hair and his mad crew, researching this info for every one of you! So get lost in the moment find yourself in the recording of T Hair's best it's all about learning! Jesus loves you! T Harrison Productions

Mister Silly you can call me Willy, I'm on the go, driving down to Philly, some of the roads get a little hilly, always prepare for the winter it gets a little chilly, you can find me at the deli filling my belly, no time for a plan b what are you trying to tell me? I'm making all this money, what are you trying to sell me?

Its 2018, here lately I been on the grind, pursuing my dreams, just spent the last nine months every day on time! Only a matter of time till they see what is right! On my way to Michigan to see my best friend, his name is Austin. We go way back, back to when we trapped for a living, we had to act for a living, we had to sack for a living, we started to rap for a living, took a lot action for a living. I remember when they would laugh at a nigga, ha-ha, I'm still laughing, nigga. I'm still rapping, nigga, massive action watch for the distractions my nigga. Look at this cash, watch me make a pass, burn you to ash for a living, lord forgive me for sinning. I'm addicted to winning, addicted to twinning, addicted to grinning, addicted to sinning. Lord forgive me, I need some healing, started at the bottom, with all this writing my label dropped, and I'm on the climb better watch out. Head down, eyes up, coming for the come up, yes I'm on the launch, looking for a rush, looking for a touch, Austin and I are about to have brunch, my homie g dog, we are raw, don't give a damn if your ten feet tall, we will beat you on the court, just playing you dog I am making rights with my wrongs, we are the captains, back to stacking. Hop in my ride, cameras inside, paparazzi outside, I say living the famous life sometimes you want to hide! High life, high on life, Lamborghini in drive cruising time, my name is Tyler I am on fire I'm climbing higher, I'm getting my lighter, I'm getting flyer, flying up with crew. T Harrison's going to tell the news, T Harrison's on the news, T Harrison is kissing a cute girl while he's on a date with her at the zoo. See, she's his honeypoo, he can kiss her when he wants because he has the moves and she stays with him because he's the best view, these other niggas don't have a clue, what it takes to be a man or wear the shoe. Blonde hair, blue eyes, yes she is fine. Ah yeah, this was supposed to be about Michigan! Chilling with my best friend! Rolling up like old times with my friends, met his grandparents for the first time, they were sweet, Miss Renee was too fly, remember ladies and gentleman if it isn't fly it isn't right if you don't grind you won't reach the gold mine! Met her husband, Michael, he was a tight guy, he wasn't shy guy, he was the right guy! Happy for both of you all! Olivia's boyfriend was headed to basic, bout to go through hell and shit. Been there before its some real shit! Rachel turned 16 growing up reminiscing about when we grew up in the streets remembering life from behind the scenes, back to before I even knew I could rap on this beat! This gift is pretty neat! I love you all, I'm going to get some sleep!

These next poems I wrote in the 6th grade in Mrs. Rakestraw's class,

The light in the sky, as it reflects down the water, wondering what it beholds tomorrow. Life would be frigid without the light, grateful that the light is everything we need to survive.

I'm like a cloud because I'm relaxed. I'm easy going and laid back. I don't let stuff ruin my day like if I get embarrassed it doesn't bother me. I go with the flow and I don't like to start trouble. I daydream and it's like I'm floating in the air. I like to be organized and clean. I'm nice and sometimes I'm hyper.

Turkey, taste like jerky, tender, sweet above all treats, eating the delicious delight at home.

Caramel apples, rich delicious. Delighting, exciting, and sighing. Brothers and I eating caramel apples. Eating, tasting, and dreaming. Sweet, yummy, mouthwatering splendid.

I Am Poem – I am quiet and I am myself. I wonder how long it will take until there's a new skate park. I hear songs in my head. I saw schools of fish at the beach. I want to be a lead singer of a heavy metal band. I am quiet and be my own self. I pretend I'm flying, I feel good. I like to touch cool material, I worry I might fail the 6th-grade. I cry when something really important happens that I love like a family member. I am quiet and I am my own self. I understand if people are tired. I say never give up. I dream I might be hanging with my friends in Texas. I try to act the best. I hope we get a dirt bike soon. I am quiet and I am my own self.

The little things inside are surely hard to find, the wonders that you wouldn't expect, come from the ones with respect.

Green gum, sweet and yummy. As I yell loudly, it's sour, chewing the delicious gumball, at home.

Five ways to look at a rose – As pollen released from the rose, the door began to close. A rose is only a rose if it grows old. The rose with pollen is wise, the rose without pollen is foolish. As the rose got cold it began to turn vibrant gold.

Archers with a bow, orange-colored crows, shark teeth, above the reef, above the depths of the ocean deep.

The 2011 Cullman Middle School Spelling Bee, this certificate is presented in recognition of Tyler Harrison for dedication to improving spelling, increasing vocabulary, learning concepts, and developing correct English usage.

Where poems hide – papers in the dresser, batteries in the computer, plugs in the wall, a skateboard that's broke, never-ending game, red candy cane, cordless phone, heavy metal song, striped shirt, yellow letter.

There once was a clock that ticked, he spoiled the fun with a click, he sang around town while making everyone frown, until one day he got very sick.

Dig a hole, under the snow; Manners are good because they are told.

- JETS
- FAST, COOL
- IN THE WORLD
- SILVER AND CHROME METAL
- ZOOMING THROUGH A BIG CLOUD, VROOM
- SILVER AND CHROME METAL
- IN THE WORLD
- FAST, COOL
- JETS

That was all of the poems I wrote in 6th-grade, below will be ones that I wrote recently.

It's by God's hand that I can move my hands. Follow his plan, be the man. Living life because I'm convinced, flowing free it's how I stand, on his holy ground is where I land. Breaking ground I am coming for the town, it's by his hand that I can comprehend, whipping down the drive all I see is posted signs, put in time and you will rise, find your mind, and reach the tide. I'm not like these other guys, I'm the real deal, can't you tell? Too good to be true, I'm here to prove, making moves it's how I groove, you can say I'm like a gorilla I'm always on the move, I will be escaping the zoo headed for the jungle before the monsoon. The mumbo jumbo some people be spitting isn't cool. Love yourself, stay in school, I will be chilling in the pool making rules, they love you for a minute, but watch for when they turn their back, they aren't true. I'm aware you losers are scared, you are coming for the top, and I am already there. Yes, I did take the stairs, climbed out the pit, God led my steps, here I am, I'm speaking now y'all got me preaching now, working two jobs, never weak, enrolled in college, chasing dreams, living life under the sea, you can call me SpongeBob cause I'm connected to my inner child, making all of this green changing scenes. I believe in make-believe. King Mickey and Donald Duck are cruising with me, cruising down the boulevard living large, going hard spitting bars, got my team. Taking charge found my passion with Christ, he gave me the gift to speak into this mic, traveling everywhere, and God is everywhere. Giving back is what I seek, listen closely please, please, identify with your gifts, develop your gifts, wrap your gifts, then give them away, you can always change your way. Getting paid I'm never late recognize real, recognize fake. These snakes don't know how to play the game, I got some words to say, you phonies watch out I do not play, my name is T Hair and love is the name for a change, watch me be great. They don't know I'm here, the beginning of fearing him, it's by God's hand that I can write what is in my head, and it is the Holy Spirit working through me. Faith in my Lord, he is my sword, I am shooting for the moon, if you want to make a report, I serve for free cause I love the Lord. I see you looking at me, I don't know what for, oh yeah that is right you see back throughout school y'all would laugh and pick on me for being different, was very cruel, the greatest revenge is massive success so who is laughing now? I got everyone's respect you all didn't know I could rap, didn't know I could trap, thankful you all respect me now, my name is Tyler Harrison, I'm from a small town, when you come to my show bet it gets loud, because I am lit, when you hear me you may trip, the frequencies and volumes that I hit. Experience the experiences, loosen your grips, living outside of the box it is how I live, ever since I was a kid, I was your friend. I love you all, can you comprehend?

Just in case you didn't, I wanted to let you in, and I didn't want us to end, and I wanted to be more than just your friend, I wanted to represent, I'm more than just a ten, and I'm more than this common sense, so why are you asking if I'm on pretend. You got me falling off on the deep end, I wonder what you're thinking, wonder what you're seeing, am I really breathing? Been having these weird thoughts lately, who am I believing in, you got to change you, got to change your sins to change your sentence, to free yourself from the wrath of these demons. Be cleansed by the blood of Christ, let the Holy Spirit in to renew your mind. Be different, be careful for the demons are here, but the angel of light guards me against their wickedness, I am a child of God, he is my defender, I am a part of his purpose to liberate these lost sinners, that they have a friend that will always let them in, his name is Jesus Christ, he is living in us, we got to invite him in our heart and let him in, if we're ever going to win this spiritual warfare that we are always in! Let Jesus be your Heavenly Father, don't believe Satan, don't be trapped by your unbelief and the lies from your sin! Choose Jesus's love today and you will always win! I love you all this is me going out in the deep end!

You see I pick up the pen, this pen is my friend because I think on paper, I don't think like them, because I open the dresser, it has multiple levels, like the levels of my mind, they are like different gears, certain words can get them rolling, when certain word enter in my mind, certain ones open, here lately I been writing a lot, spending two hours every day on this novel to plot, to stretch my imagination, to let you all in for a lot, sacrificing my time to rhyme better with thoughts, to amaze you all that this boy is giving all of his guts, so here I go matching with my flow, I don't care for the competition I came to dominate the road, I came to breathe life into these lost souls, by through generosity I can release my foes, see Jesus says it shall be as heaping coals on my enemies heads, when I do good deeds for them and love them with the rest. For every action that I take to serve them, I'm serving him, like a brother or sister brings new life to treat them as the best. Love your enemies, do good to those that persecute you, for you make your Daddy proud. Did you know that God loves you as much as he loves your enemies? For he created you both from dust, that he may gain our love, and rescue us from the tycoon. To wrap us in his chest before he comes through, as a roaring lion comes through to martyr the lives of lost people, don't think he won't eat you too. Live for Christ, have eternal life with him. Put on the whole armor of God, so the Devil can't take a hold of your life, love your Heavenly Father for he gave up the ultimate sacrifice, his one, and only son so that he may gain our love. Redeem us from the price, if you walk away from him, he will leave the 99 to come after the one in the darkest of nights.

That boy can preach, that boy can teach, that boy can sink his teeth into the word as if he's sinking them into a peach, that boy can have the whole congregation falling to its knees, by letting the Holy Spirit possess his body and death fall at his feet, that boy can change lives by what he speaks, open eyes by what he sings, see God gives us all gifts to set each other free. We are here to encourage one another, it is what Jesus did preach, to uplift one another when their world's falling to pieces, to be a friend to them in their time of need. Lord, I don't know where this road is taking me but I will follow thee, for you gave me this life, you hold the keys, when my life is over you will pull the keys out of the ignition, my soul will leave this body and I will be convicted, it is what Jesus did for us at the Cross at the Crucifixion, Thank you for your love that you shed for me, I will follow you all of my days, you can always hold the key.

My brother said I have a creative mind, he said don't waste your time getting distracted by these distractions, that you encounter online. Develop your gift, empower people's lives, for you are one in a million you can rhyme any rhyme, today is my Declaration of Independence. I'm using my gifts to bring repentance for we were all once lost sinners but there is one man that was sinless, he wasn't just a man, he was an immortal God in the flesh. Sent here to take our place by dying on the cross, He saved our ways even though we still fail him every day, so God I give you my lust for the corruption for it causes destruction, it will bring you to your knees rendering all that you got. It will eat up your fruit, for you will rust on the inside, destroying you too. Bring life into your life, bring happiness into your eyes, and bring the joy and love of serving yourself and others, being washed in the blood, inviting the Holy Spirit into your life. For we are made of dust but it is his covenant with us, he is a must for us to be connected with God in Jesus we must trust. For we are at war between good and evil, let Jesus and his angels fight for your rights, letting the spirit amplify your heights, depositing your belief, pull out your bible for it is Christ that I have my degree! Call on your Heavenly Father and you will always be on the ball!

I found my old bible, it reminded me to when I went to my first revival, and it was when I first stepped out of the crowd to get baptized. I believed in Jesus with all of my heart, all of my sins were washed away and I was redeemed by his sacrifice! Representing my faith, representing my grades, representing that I will make the play, I will make the change by planting seeds of life into every human being, with the insight of information that flows from the light, I will be the light just like Christ that burns in the darkest of nights. I remember when I had no ties, had to get up to pay the price, elevated, hell of faded, so high on the holy spirit, I am a walking elevator, walking down road, walking through the doors, meeting people I have never met before, first time being on the Ellen DeGeneres show, nice to meet you, I am a poet, thankful you let me show it, from this platform I can grow it, check out my book it is on the come up, back in the day, they would laugh, now I'm making cash, now you can watch me act, T Harrison is the name and I am not going back, I'm letting out the facts, I'm open-minded it is how I rap, DJ Khaled can rack, he doesn't know I am here, I been rhyming for ten years, mainstream can't you hear, I will not be trapped by fear, if you aren't on the team I am not listening. I am setting up my time I can flow with any rhyme, I can sign any sign I can see any sign, it by the precious blood that I'm alive, prayed for wisdom in the darkest of times, I call on Jesus to fight my fights, I am a disciple for Christ, I will preach until then end of my life, while making you all look fly, doing your hair and speaking in your mind. I love you Jesus and I love your people, even if they don't know you, if they encounter me, they will that's a fact, see the man with big dreams will always stack, typing on these keys, making it out of these streets, I had to get my degree for it changed me, for it made me who I am for it opened my mind to sell, the information flowed through me, went from default to hairstylist. Now I am serving hundreds every day, with every single client it phases me, it tangles me in the presence, and for I am living the opportunity and I will confess it! I love you all this is T Hair wrapping you another present!

This is the takeover, this is the makeover, this is the first cover, I am writing on a land rover, flexing with my shoulders you can call me Frodo, I don't think they know though, I am from a fairyland, I am speaking with my hands,

I am reaching out for the plan, on a long quest, it has been so long since I been home, not even sure where it is, T Harrison on the beat, this journey didn't come free, let freedom in, let's choose love and we will always win, lifting off, five, four, three, two, one, shaking the dead weight off, it feels great to be climbing the highest rocks, never would have dreamed of meeting The Rock, I met him in my dream last night that was so awesome! Snowboarding, going down slopes, yes I'm jumping rope, yes I'm wearing warm clothes, adrenaline pumping, endorphins rushing, dopamine crushing, the feeling I get from operating in a peak state every morning! Compares to none, I am one of the ones!

I have learned that when I bite the bullet it doesn't hurt as bad as I thought it would, every time the reward is always greater than the sacrifice to receive it! As I sit here and wonder, as I sit here and ponder, piece by piece my life flows in order, sheet by sheet these words are like mortars, going off in my mind, the signs I have seen, the miracles that have changed me, for if you don't believe in miracles, you probably have never lived one. As I sit here and think, as I lay down and dream, as I open up every door that has closed on me, it is only then do I start to see, for they closed before but now I can open all things, the words that I find in my mind, I'm not sure how they get placed there, but it is heavenly and miraculous, I believe God is dropping bits and pieces of wisdom in my mind every day, he created my soul so he can do all things, his spirit lives in me so I can do all things, invite his spirit by believing in him and you can have the power of Christ work through you too. I can achieve every dream for I believe, I will always see, see the haters can't see, blinded by the system but they can't blind me, they are at the bottom, I can hear them scream, their voices echo up this mountain, it is so green. I climbed it with my own two hands that God left with me; it is with these hands that he set me free. I am always climbing, I am always rhyming, it is all about your timing, it is all about the signs, please watch for the kind things, for one small act of kindness can create a paradox in time, changing all things, always choose love, set your loved ones free, by choosing compassion to take action forget about the distractions, don't lose your passion, for you are one in a million and I am a million in one, so here I speak I love, don't grow weak, choose our God above to reach every peak, to plant and harvest every seed, growing a beautiful life of service, sacrifice, and loving everything. Love the journey, love your dreams, this is T Harrison flowing.

Writing, your gift of perceiving the world with such a creative mind, the way you dress is a gift for me because I think you pick out the cutest outfits that I want to take off. Singing, you have such a beautiful voice, it's is as if you sound like you aren't really human but a descendant from Heaven with harmony like that. Your Turner's is a gift it is how you look at it, you can impact millions of people's lives with your story. I like to think of mental illness as a gift in certain cases cause it allows us to see the world in a different way, also there isn't anything wrong with being sensitive for the more honed in you are on your senses, the more you can sense what is real. Your personality is a gift, your personal reality, the way that you see the world based on your values, and beliefs. The fact that you are breathing right now and so many parts of your body are functioning without even thinking about it. It is a gift, your non-striated movements, how you can think then act, you have the ability to choose, that is what separates us from every creature the power of choice. You even play instruments so beautifully Lucy.

We would wonder through the night, we would wonder through our eyes. We would climb a tree together with a cooling wind that gives us goose bumps causing us to hold each other close in disguise. The tree is so large, the night is so blue, Lord help us to be strong when our time is through, but I don't want to let you go, I want to sit next to you on this branch forever, watching the lightning bugs glow, and to listen to you tell me stories about your shows, for cupid must have shot us when we got close, that is okay for what a blessing it is to explore with your soul, to adventure with you as I kiss you on the nose for it is so cute and we are also. Do you see the flowers in the yard? Red, green, and blue, all of the fairies floating around, it's easy to see that this isn't our normal reality, We are operating in our dreams, the pixie dust does flow, just as this poem goes on, so does this realm of magic unfolds, for this world, only few can see, only the gifted special ones can create anything. For I am trapped in a world of unordinary things, In a blink, your eyes catch me with your stare, in a moment, I am with you in your arms, already there, you hold me in your heart, for you are aware, that even when we are apart, I am still there. Your hair is ruby red, silky smooth like a red velvet dress, oh how vibrant your face is for it turns red, when I kiss your lips, running my fingers through your hair, how we run off to a magical palace, when we adventure into the parts of our mind, that we have never been. You carry

87

me, and I carry you for you are so special and I am so crazy about you.

"As we sit here in the tree, I will let you dive into my journal of notes and places that I've seen. Course material in school that really interested me, Lucy, I'm sure you will find it mesmerizing for I am letting you in my world of convoluted scenes."

"Tyler, oh how a joy it is to digest and grow with all the information that I read, oh how I find myself cohering with your peace. For you and I still choose happiness regardless of the past, you and I still choose love and forgiveness for it is the only way to move forward, past the past."

"Lucy here are some notes, I recorded some content I learned in my psychology class, I really think you will enjoy reading them."

Disturbed emotions, Inconsistent with reality, Gets in the way of us reaching our goals.

Activating event, Belief, Consequence

Irrational belief – doesn't help you reach your goals. When I can't control my emotions, I am probably addicted to that emotion.

I started this journal in January of 2017, my first semester back in college when I took Psychology as a class, which I fell in love with the study of the way our minds work. I have recorded a lot of notes and thoughts in this which I will share with you all.

Formal operational – Abstract thinking, concrete thinking,

We are born with a lifetime supply of Neurons, at three years old, synapses form based on early experiences. At age 15 years old, our mind is finely tuned to the environment.

Too little stimulation is bad; more TV equals more attention problems, depending on the content being consumed.

Studies in neuroplasticity – the brain's adaptability, has proved that repeated experiences actually change the physical structure of the brain. Discipline is about teaching, not about punishment. Finding ways to teach children the correct way to act is essential for healthy development. Children have a profound need for connection. When children are overtaxed emotionally they sometimes misbehave. Misbehavior is often a cry for help, calming down, and a bid for connection. When the parental response is to isolate the child, an instinctual psychological need of the child goes unmet. Brain imaging shows that the experience of relational pain, similar to the cause of rejection – looks very similar to the experience of physical pain in terms of brain activity. Putting your child in time out is damaging the brain, could cause anxiety, or social phobia in life.

Fetal alcohol syndrome is very bad, it can cause brain damage to the baby. It also increases the chance of it having learning disabilities or ending up in a mental institution or even in jail.

The need to sleep is one of the strongest biological urges we have. Humans use about ten percent less energy when they're sleeping.

Moral intuition, judgments on what is right and wrong, moral action, necessary steps it takes to transform, the will to do the right thing.

Toxic stress, not having adult support that every child needs, early adversity can cause autoimmunity to change, therefore disease set in. That is how I believe I got this autoimmune disease in my eyes.

Beauty can be found anywhere, as long as we have our senses at least one of them, we have a possibility that allows us to feel human. Let death be what takes us not lack of imagination.

At times we aren't likely to experience what it is like to raise multiple children in a village; our generation is about waking up to whom we really are, and what we are here to create. We have to get really clear on one thing. Tapping into our strengths and engaging in them is one of the greatest ways to attract the kinds of people you need in your life. To bless and inspire others and build a sense of community in ways that fill rather than drain you.

Being homosexual, the gene can develop in the DNA before the child is born. Majorities of schools do not want to teach sex education. In eight states in the USA, there are laws that limit what teachers can say about being homosexual.

Apes lack theory of mind. Stay human, stay curious.

Perception is what was useful to our past. A boat enables to see other parts of the country that can be unknown to us. The future is putting the digital world into the real world. Boredom is an emotion that is a less intense version of disgust. Boredom pushes away from low stimulus situations.

Sometimes stimulation, any stimulation is perceived as better than none at all. We as humans do not like being bored at all. The mind is a good thing to lose ever so often. Some people choose isolation to learn from isolation. He who travels furthest travels with others.

The relationship between brain activity and conscious experiences is still a mystery. We have misinterpreted our perceptions before because it looked that way. Galileo says, "I think that tastes, odors, colors, and so on reside in consciousness. Hence if the living creature were removed all of the qualities would be annihilated." About ⅓ of the brain's cortex is in vision. We have blind spots because it lies in the structure of our eye. Inside of it, there is a set of photosensitive cells. Just like film paper responds to incoming light, it gives out signals for the light to see. They communicate with several neurons that begin to process this information. Then the information is sending off to the brain through the optic nerve. The light and the information coming from the front of the eye have to go through the film. There's a spot on the film where all the information goes through the optic nerve.

Speakers use air to push molecules to make sound. Some frequencies get pushed the wrong way sometimes. Our brains are so good at finding patterns, that sometimes it does it subconsciously.

Genetic engineering will affect everyone. It can cure cancer and diseases. It could also lead to modifying humans, it may even extend our life expectancy.

Entanglement is something Einstein didn't like, even on his dying day, he believed that quantum mechanics was wrong because it included entanglement. Entanglement comes from one simple equation, what it means, in theory, is one equally – simple consequence. Newton's idea is that if you want to predict the future, you write down an equation about what you want to do in the world. The equation allows you to turn the crank mathematically and predict what's going to happen when you do that in the world. That is why it is important to model what works.

Working memory has four basic components, it allows us to store some immediate experiences and a little bit of knowledge. It allows us to reach back into our long-term memory, pulls some of that in case we need it. It mixes it and processes it for our current goal. Working memory capacity has a lot of positive effects. People who optimize this tend to be good storytellers and good at standardized testing. They're able to have high levels of writing ability and able to reason at high levels. Working memory is limited in capacity, duration, and focus. We are meaning, making machines, what we process we learn. If we aren't processing were not living life. Memory is suggestive, subjective, and malleable.

Humans apply – Mechanical muscles make human labor less in demand, so are mechanical minds making brain labor less in demand. Better technology makes much better jobs for humans. Technology gets better, faster, sharper, and cheaper at rate biology can't match. Just as the car was the beginning of the end for the horse, so now the car shows us the shape of things to come. Automation is inevitable.

Sunk Cost Fallacy – What you've already spent in the past. Making a choice not based on what outcome you think is going to be. The best going forward but instead based on a desire not to see your past investment go to waste. Having the opportunity to push past that and make better choices instead will end up being a better outcome for your future.

The illusion of truth – the things we are exposed to repeatedly seems truer due to cognitive ease. Individuals with more brain activity learn slower than those with less brain activity. Overthinkers may learn tasks more slowly and be less successful at those tasks versus those who don't analyze and evaluate their every move.

Language is a window into social relations. Language has to do with two things; it's got to convey some content such as bribe, command, and proposition. It has to negotiate a relationship type. The solution to use language at two levels, literal form and politeness are a simple example. Human relationships across the world's culture, each prescribes a distinct way of distributing resources. Each has a distinct evolutionary basis, each applies most naturally to certain people.

Princeton University shows that the mental demand of not having a flush bank account can suppress cognitive function by 15 IQ points. This potentially leads to bad decisions that keep the cycle of poverty spinning along. A 1993 study from the University of Michigan showed that children living in poverty tend to have lower IQ regardless of their parent's IQ or marital status.

Awareness is a conscious connection with universal intelligence. Instead of being lost in your thinking, when you are awake you recognize yourself as the awareness behind it. This is pretty cool to think about. Living up to an image that you have of yourself or that other people have of you is inauthentic living.

Addiction is due to the disconnection of those around us. We are going to have to change the unnatural way we live and rediscover each other. The opposite of addiction is not sobriety, the opposite of addiction is connection.

Focus on the task at hand; minimize multiple distractions by turning off the phone or TV. Coordination is built with repetitions whether correct or incorrect. If you gradually increase the speed of the quality repetitions, you have a better chance of doing them correctly. Effective practice is the best way we have to push our individual limits achieving new heights and maximizing our potential.

We are fascinated by interaction, body language is communication. We are also influenced by nonverbal, our thoughts, our feelings, and our physiology. Our nonverbal govern how other people think and feel about us. Our nonverbal govern subconsciously how we think and feel about ourselves as well without us realizing it unless we are aware of it. Our minds change our bodies, but do our bodies change our minds? The answer is yes, you could be feeling down in your mind but if choose to smile regardless, you will find yourself experiencing happiness. It is by power that we react to stress. The body can shape the mind as well as role changes can change the mind.

Once you get above Rudimentary Cognitive skill, rewards don't matter. Higher incentives lead to worse performance. Three factors lead to better performance and personal satisfaction. Autonomy, Mastery, and Purpose, Autonomy is our desire to be self-directed. If you want engagement, self-direction is better in the workplace. One day of autonomy produces things that never emerge. Mastery is our ability to get better at the craft we are developing.

Higher knowledge is often used by spiritually-minded people to describe important but hard to reach mental states. As human beings, we spend most of our lives functioning in states of lower consciousness. Higher consciousness is a huge triumph over the primitive mind.

All kids have the extreme talent and we squander them. Creativity is as important now in education as literacy, and we should treat it with the same status. If you're not prepared to be wrong, you will never come up with anything original. Picasso says all children are born artists, the problem is to remain one as we grow up. Creativity is the process of having original ideas that have value, intelligence is distinct.

What makes you comfortable can ruin you, what makes you uncomfortable is the only way to grow. What dictates the size of a goldfish is its environment. Learn to embrace discomfort, life wasn't created to be what we think it is. We must experience the wilderness to be taught what cannot be otherwise known. Order is what we shall fear the most because it is a threat.

Stress's purpose was once designed to save us. What once helped us survive has become the scourge of our lives. A baboon's rank determines the level of stress hormone in his system. In the dominant male, you can expect your stress hormone to be low. If you are submissive, in the group with the low rankers, the have nots have increased heart rates and higher blood pressure. Our positions in work as humans are similar to those of baboons. When stressed the body begins shutting down all nonessential systems including the immune system, during this stomach bacteria can run amuck. Stress can cause ulcers by disrupting our body's ability to heal itself. Social and psychological stress can clog your arteries, restrict blood flow, and jeopardize the health of our heart. That is just the beginning of stress's deadly curse. Chronic stress can kill brain cells, stress can make us feel plain misery. Stress can be the reason for global obesity. Stress may damage us long before we are aware. The absence of stress can impact society. The same is true for humans.

The brain size is three pounds of tofu-like tissue, 1.1 trillion brain cells, and 100 billion "gray matter" neurons. It is always on 24/7 365 days a year, instant access to information on demand, 20-25% of blood flow, oxygen, and glucose. Neurons firing around five to fifty times a second (or faster), signals crossing your brain in a tenth or a hundredth of a second, a typical neuron makes 5,000 connections, 500 trillion synapses. Our mind equals a flow of information within the nervous system. Our brain equals a necessary, proximal sufficient condition for the mind. As your brain changes, your mind changes, as your mind changes your brain, it changes the principal activities of brains are making changes in themselves. The education of attention would be an education par excellence. The amygdala is primed to label experiences negatively. Compassion is the wish that someone doesn't suffer combined with sympathetic concern. If you take care of the minutes, the years will take care of themselves with wisdom and contentment.

Approach, Gratitude, Peace, Love, Affiliate, Avoid – Good example of defense mechanism – Acting prideful, it is one of the ways we repress what's in our subconscious mind, in our dichotomy and duality. We repress things we are uncomfortable with.

The results of people suffering from mental illness are crazy. So many people in the U.S can't get treatment or don't because they don't have healthcare. I don't see why the U.S doesn't replicate a system similar to Germany's healthcare system. It is mind-boggling how mental illness has affected this world so much. Our whole system needs an overhaul.

This is what addiction feels like, everything is great at first, but after a while it is lonesome and you end up lost in your head. Depression is frightening but you are not alone.

Mindfulness, finding our inner peace every day, taking in this moment and shutting our thoughts off, can beat depression, Mindfulness may be a new choice for millions of people with recurring depression on repeat prescriptions. Antidepressant medication is the key treatment for preventing relapse, reducing the likelihood of relapse or recurrence by up to two thirds when taken correctly. Serotonin affects the growth of brain cells. Depression is a disease. Depression has opened me up to becoming though by amplifying what it truly means to love and serve for when I do take these actions the symptoms disappear, Depression was a portal to a spiritual passage for me. Everyone will face depression at some point in their lives. The world is alive, we have to live an inspired life to live the most satisfying life.

For a lot of people, it is clearer to build a good career than inner character. 50% of our parents that live to 85 will have dementia. Groups doing aerobic exercises had an increase in the hippocampus which helped with memory. Our hippocampus shrinks with age but we can fight the aging of it with exercise. Having a better brain can help you think more clearly. Learn more easily, remember more, build better relationships and unlock potential for us in the future. The brain can change, if your brain can change, your life can change. Exercising is one of the best ways to do it!

Psychiatric disorders are caused by chemical imbalances in the brain. Psychiatric illnesses are disorders of emotion circuit function. Neurosurgery comes from a long tradition, it has been around for 7,000 years. In Mesoamerica, there was neurosurgery taking place. People thought that if you had a neuro or psych problem that you were possessed by a spirit. Different parts of the brain do different things. 1,000 years ago patients survived brain surgery but had to live with huge holes in their heads. The practice finally came to an end when the Spanish arrived in the 16th century and decided to make it illegal.

Don't get so caught up in the world that you forget about the one that created it! There is power in the name of Jesus!

Climbing down the ladder, swimming in the breeze, watch me shatter, what's the matter, laughter, laughter, you can call me the mad hatter, I am faster, I am past her, she's a disaster, white as Casper, I'm a pastor, delivering is how I test her, watch for the 5-0 they are tracking, I am underground, I come from way down, I had to break, I had to shake mounds, I had to take towns, walking in the dark, walking with my heart, talking about my part, this flow is an art, okay here I go blue hoodie that's for sure when you see me at my show, stop, look very close, it is funny for me because I have seen you before but I don't know who you are, you are phonies, you aren't my homies, I got an army, they aren't foreign, they were with me ever since the morning, ever since my mourning, I had to warn them for whatever you do to me I will record, this is my report, this is my chord, this is my port, there are no shortcuts in this game, if you want it all you better start, if you want to be tall you better call on the Lord, for you will face many trials and tribulations, don't get scared for you got to walk through the fire to experience getting through the door, you have to lay it all down to pick up the right things to trade it all in for the bright rings, for I don't even have a degree in writing but my Heavenly Father put these words inside of me, to share with you all it's his dream, it is why I am here is to lead you all into unlocking your dreams, for we all have dreams that he gave to us with the power to achieve to wear every ring. To get in the ring with the darker parts of your mind, to put them down in the ground for they are brainwashing, don't let the demons talk you out of who you were created to be called on Jesus, call on things that are not, see the invisible, destroy the enemy that peeks through the window, Holy Water, hold me God, Holy God, Holy One, guide with me your rod, take the lead for sure, calling on my angels 'cause I can't do it anymore, Jesus will make the way, Jesus will save the day, Jesus can heal all things, no matter who is president Jesus is always king. Walking in your presence, living for your presence, I don't care who is president for God, you are Heaven sent, created so you can cleanse me from my sin, thank you, Lord, for saving me, thank you, God, for planting the seeds of literacy in my mind above all things, thank you God that I can still see and this disease in my eyes hasn't taken a hold of me, robbing me from my vision, but as long as I can hear and speak, I can still let them in, into the depths of my mind, allowing them to adventure into the beauty of your mind that you created for me, not only did he do this for me, but he did it for you. Open your mind, let him through, let him take a hold of you, ride the roller coaster of truth, it can be rocky but without the hardships, you can't have the best views. I can feel the fire calling out, this is something I have to do, to step into a new level, to see double. To bless everyone while remaining humble, there is great music in all of us, it is up to us to unlock it, and I haven't revealed this music to anyone except my novel!

As I read out these pages, as I stand on these stages, as the air grows hazy, from the fog lights I just hope they can still understand me, for I am juggling this story that has caused me to go on tour, never would have dreamed of getting on board with America's finest, I'm recording, I'm resorting to all this information in my head for it is not corny, this is the tour, Lucy, I couldn't find her but she still is important, she has been in mourning, I found her in the morning she was sitting in a forest filled with fairies from New Orleans, coasting, rowing, sailing this ship to the court, writing every report, rocking some Jordan's, it's time to step on stage, it is time to be great, I am always on time I am never late, started at the bottom, that is okay, for if you find out what you love you will find a way, to finish the race to live with grace tasting all of these gourmet places first time eating with celebrities I am the craziest, I am the one, no I am not conceited I'm just having fun rapping, spitting and living, loving and giving, changing people's lives as I pull the lever, I will never give into the sellouts, I will always carry out every mission with pride, this is T Hair speaking loud I love you all this is what I'm about!

I figured out why Marshall Mathers referred to himself as Eminem or Slim Shady for these were the higher parts of his mind that he tapped into in order to creatively express himself, sort of like how I refer to myself as T Harrison for it is higher part of life that lives in me that allows me to write.

For honesty is the best policy, don't do life alone call on the one who created you, a relationship with our Heavenly Father, let him be a guide to you, let him be your shoulder to cry on for when you take a wound, let him wrap you in his arms for we are his little children and that is what he wants to do, always remember he loved you so much, he thought of you when he spoke you into existence, you were special for sure, please don't let the demons corrupt you for they will drag your spirit around chaining you to the room, as a lost puppet it will get darker and darker and before you know it you will run out of room, you will have a permanent mindset and the enemy will run you, choose love today call on Jesus, fly with him, glide with him, climb with him, sign with him, let his voice enter into the inner parts of you for it is his timing, we all live for eternity it is up to us to decide where we want to call home, where we want to reside in.

I have to keep writing, I have to keep fighting, I have to keep being led by the Holy Spirit, I have to keep an open mind and I can't let these doubters come between who I am, for who I am is who I'm called to be, who I'm called to be is an influencer, who saves these people from danger, for there is so many people in the world filled with anger, they will take it out on you just to destroy before you make it out of the manger, the hatred I can't bear for out of it is a poison that will corrupt your every hair, for you will rot before you are aware and as a carcass that walks around people will tend to stare, for you let the evil in, you let the darkness win, you didn't call on Jesus to fight your battles to cleanse you from your sins, to cover you with his hands for we are in a

101

spiritual warfare that I can't understand, for I just want to choose love and happiness but these demons keep on trying to settle in, I rebuke you all for it won't be long and my Jesus will cast you all back to where you live, it is in that lake of fire where you won't be able to lay a hand, on God's little children for we are here to dominate his land, to represent Christ in a world that is covered in a blanket of darkness, us as believers are a candle in the wind, a flower in the field, a twinkle in time, but these words will last again, until the end of time, they will be written on a plaque, carved in stone, sitting on the stand for even when the hurricanes come they will always stand. With Jesus, you will always land on his Holy Ground regardless of the clans, that try to tear down on your mission for they laugh now, but don't let it in they are the mockers, it is what they do. They are the shockers, they will pull out every weapon from of their arsenal to bury you, to puff them self-up, while contemplating the truth, letting the darkness overtake them but you can't be defeated for you regarded as the moment of truth for you have the fruits of the spirit you will always stand in truth.

As I sit here and wonder, as I sit here and ponder, piece by piece my life flows together back in order, sheet by sheet, these words are like mortars going off in my mind, the signs I have seen, the miracles that have changed me, for if you don't believe in miracles, you probably have never lived one. As I sit here and think, as I lay down and dream, as I open up every door that has closed on me, it is only then do I start to see, for they closed on me before, but now I can open all things, the words that I find in my mind, I'm not sure how they got placed there, but it is heavenly and miraculous, I believe God is dropping bits and pieces of wisdom in my mind every day, he created my soul so he can do all things, his spirit lives in me so I can do all things, invite his spirit by believing in him and so can you, I can achieve every dream for I believe, I will always see, see the haters can't see, that is why they scream, because they are at the bottom and I can't hear their voices from this mountain so green, I climbed it with my own two hands, that God left with me, which set me free, I am always climbing, always rhyming, it is all about timing, it is all about the signs, please watch for the kind things, for one small act of kindness can create a paradox in time, changing all things, always choose love, set your loved ones free, :) with compassion take action with the distractions, don't lose your passion, for you are one in a million and I am a million in one, so here I speak I love, don't grow week, choose our God above to reach every peak, love the journey, love your dreams, this is T Harrison flowing :)

I have learned that when I bite the bullet, it doesn't hurt as bad as I thought it would.

My brother said, I have a creative mind. He said, don't waste your time getting distracted by these distractions that you encounter online, develop your gift empower people's lives for you are one in million for you can rhyme any rhyme today is my declaration of independence I'm using my gift to bring repentance for we're all lost sinners but there's one man that was sinless, wasn't just a man, he was an immortal God, sent here to take our place by dying on the cross he saved our ways he even though I still fail him every day, so God I give you my lust for the corruption it causes, it will eat through your fruit and cause you to rust therefore be washed in the blood for we are made of dust but is his covenant with us, that is a must for us to be connected with God in him we can always trust

In a blink, your eyes catch me with your stare, in a moment, I am with you in your arms, already there, you hold me in your heart, for you are aware, that even when we are apart, I am still there. Your hair is ruby red, silky smooth like a red velvet dress, oh how vibrant your face is for it turns red, when I kiss your lips, running my fingers through your hair, how we run off to a magical place, when we adventure into the parts of our mind, that we have never been, you carry me and I carry you for you are so special and I am so crazy about you ⍰

You see, I pick up the pen, the pen is my friend because I think on paper I don't think like them because I open the dresser, it has multiple levels, like the levels of my mind, they are like different gears, certain words can get them rolling, when certain words enter in my mind, certain ones open, here lately I been writing a lot, spending two hours every day on this novel to plot, to stretch my imagination, to let you all in for a lot, sacrificing my time to rhyme better with thoughts, to amaze you all that this boy is giving all that he has, so here I go matching with my flow, I don't care for the competition, I came to dominate the road, I came to breathe life into these lost souls, by through generosity I can release my foes, see Jesus says it shall be as heaping coals on my enemies heads, when I do good deeds for them and love them with the rest, for every action that I take to serve them I'm serving him like a brother or sister brings new life to treat them as the best. Love your enemies, do good to those that persecute you, for you make your daddy proud, did you know God loves your enemy as much as he loves you? For he created you both from dust, that he may gain our love and rescue us from the tycoon, to wrap us in our chest before he comes through, as a roaring lion comes through to martyr the lives of lost people, don't think he won't eat you too, live for Christ, live the best life, put on the armor of God, so the devil can't take a hold of your life, love your Heavenly Father for he gave up the ultimate sacrifice, his one, and only son so that he gain our love and redeem us from the price, of walking away from him, he comes after us in the darkest of nights!

That boy can preach, that boy can teach, that boy can sink his teeth in the word as if he's sinking them in a peach, that boy can have the whole congregation falling to its knees, by letting the holy spirit possess his body and death fall at his feet, that boy can change lives by what he speaks, open eyes by what he sings, see God gives us all gifts to set each other free, we are to encourage one another, it is what Jesus did preach, to uplift one another when their worlds falling apart, to be a friend to them in their time of need Lord I don't know where this road is taking me but I will follow thee, for you gave me this life, you hold the keys, when my life is over you will pull the keys out ignition, my soul will leave this body and I will be convicted, but it is your precious blood that covers the angelic symbols of sins that I committed, what Jesus did for us at the cross at the crucifixion. Thank you for your love that you shed for me, I will follow you all of my days, you can always hold the key.

Just in case you didn't, I wanted to let you in, and I didn't want us to end, and I wanted to be more than just your friend. I wanted to represent, I'm more than just a ten, and I'm more than this common sense, so why you asking why I'm on pretend? You got me falling off the deep end, I'm wondering what you're thinking, wonder what you're seeing, am I really breathing? Been having these weird thoughts lately, who am I believing in; you got to change you got sins to change your sentence, to free yourself from the wrath of these demons. Be cleansed by the blood of Christ; let Holy Spirit in to renew your mind. Be different, be careful for the demons are here, but the angel of light guards me against their wickedness, I am a child of God, he is my defender, I am apart his purpose to liberate these lost sinners, that they have a friend that will always let them in, his name is Jesus Christ, he is living in us, we got to invite him in our heart and let him in, if we're ever going to win this spiritual warfare that we are always in! Let Jesus be your Heavenly Father don't believe Satan, don't be trapped by your unbelief and the lies from your sin! Choose Jesus's love today and you will always win! I love you all this is me going out in the deep end!

I could run, jump, scream and sigh but I can't get you off my mind...I could journey through the day, pretending that I'm fine, but even you know truth...When I'm without you, I am not alright...You have the prettiest blue eyes, they are blue just like the sky and when you are walking by I am possessed by the twinkle in your eyes...If you weren't so shy I would fall asleep in your arms every night, if it was up to me you would be mine, I can't seem to let you go for without you I'm a carving in stone, a story that only you can complete for we were made to grow old. I could tell you that I love you but those words have an empty ring but I could show you that I love you by letting you deep inside my dreams. For Kenzie you are an angel, you are not a scheme, you are more than what they perceive, and you are my diamond ring. 💍💍

I feel like this guy in this movie Dinner for Schmucks he is such a creative soul and people tend to question his intelligence for being so creative and being a dreamer who is truly searching for happiness who is motivated by his craft and gifts and wants to be loved

It is very attractive same here! Rosy red lips, she makes my heart jump and skip, for I haven't even met her but I want to kiss her lips, for I haven't even felt her but I want to feel her grip, for when she tugs at my heart, she unlocks the script, that unlocks me as I taste her kiss.

You will always be a part of my life; you will always be recorded in my mind, holding weight for I wrote about you, even if you never become my wife. I will always love you and we will be just fine, even if you are across the blue ocean in England, drinking on some wine, all you have to do is open up the novel, and maybe you won't cry for this is yours and my story for I wrote about our lives 💜

Even if we never get to be complete you will always hold a key that unlocks me

I suggest you not roast me, for I will drop you in the toaster, I will aim for the stars, for I am the closest, I'm sailing up the coast, for I have seen the posers, lining up on the roller coasters, they be going down, while T Hair is making all these postings, for when they didn't believe, for when they couldn't perceive, I was conceiving my dreams, like a wet dream, I was creating them all like a sex scene, got bread and butter, for I am a hunter, you can find me in the woods, chilling with my brothers, you can find me writing in my notes yeah, for I'm walking through this forest, all I see is green, for before I even turned 23, I started planting seeds. five years later now I'm owning every dream, for these phonies never win, because they don't believe in make-believe, see art is a gift, art has a twist, art can open your mind, while letting them all get lost in the mist, the return of the rhymes, the return for my life, it happened when I picked up the pen, and revived your souls back to life, recited these poems out of sight, tippy toed off the trail, journeying in the night as a holocaust man, who found life in his wife, who gave up all his love while staring her in the eyes, he said I do, to always protect you, for even when they come, I will make it through, for this mission is complex, I still remember living in them projects, see a rose can grow anywhere as long as you take care of the soil, invest in your mind, invest in your life, inspire every person you connect with, no matter what the sacrifice, for your love for them will win every fight for you are the special young king for you know how to write, T Hair

Falling is the only out I see, and I don't want to take you down with me. Don't want you take on the burden, as you follow my lead, if you do, your oxygen will slowly decrease, you will sink, as you fight to breathe, the current will pull you under as you drown with me, I may be lost in this sea, but see the land is never far, it is never out of reach, for as long as you can see, you can get there and maximize your dreams. Calling is the only route for me, freefalling is the only time I scream, and for it is the only way my lungs can really peak. I didn't mean to burn you, when I talk I speak, these words can be like coal they are very powerful, they can affect your soul, for when I think I dream, I don't want you to experience the hurt of being crushed by these demons. They can knock you down, but don't let them steal your dreams, wrap up your fists in linen, soak them in holy water, get back up on your feet, defend your life, knock those spirits in their crooked teeth. You possess the power of the Holy Spirit, you can address the power to sink these things, for if you walk by my side, you got to believe, it is the only way you will win this battle, see one day all these demons will go extinct, they will burn in the lake of fire, as we're chilling with the King. For there is a light that will never go out in our heart, it is the light God planted in you and me, as his little children, he will prepare everything we need, when the time is right until then we will pray upon our knees. For he has saved our life, an immortal God that we are created by, it is his precious blood that reigns over us, it is always Jesus in disguise!

First time coming into the program, I couldn't even speak. Surrounded by all these women and teachers, I couldn't even breathe, I didn't know how to talk to them, and they didn't know how to talk to me, many of the girls questioned me asking, "Are you gay and if not why did you choose cosmetology?"

I would reply, "No, I'm not gay and this dream chose me."

I would have never dreamed of having the opportunity to change the way people see, by changing the way they look I can influence and plant seeds, it is such a powerful craft being able to be a part of such an amazing team, at first I was shy but after being welcomed with love after the first couple tries, I truly came alive. I fell in love with doing hair, Mrs. Moore and Mrs. Flanigan took me from default to stylist, I was always there, an underdog in the field, I had to keep it real, pay attention to every detail, following every drill, crawling through this maze with a blindfold on, doing everything I could to try and hold on, my instructors were my lifesavers that pushed me along, even when some of the girls and I didn't get along, I was still there for them, I been here to follow my dreams, I been consistent for their is power in consistency, persevering through every hardship, that is what transformed me, as a hot mold, I molded into who I was created to be, a hair stylist that has the gifts of literacy, multi gifted now, more valuable, chasing more dreams. One more down, these dreams are choosing me. Onto 2nd semester, Mrs. Flanigan took the lead, as an underdog in the field, they always breathed their life into me, prepared my wings. For they strengthened me, they always believed in me even when my parents didn't, their opinions held more weight over me, for I may not be related to them, but they have always loved me…I got to participate in Skills USA, brought home the Cosmetology Quiz Bowl Championship, making progress, for I believe, that I have the power to speak it into existence, before I even blink, for afterwards I will witness it come to pass. For I am now in my 4th semester, where my eyes are wide open, I can see the light, for I am at the end of the tunnel in this day to day fight, about to make the dive, through to the other side, I made it to the end, with the help of God and my friends, he gave me this drive, to hold on through the darkest of nights, climbing up the mountain, I love being challenged for when there is no challenge, there is no growth, when there is no growth, we will all grow old, when we grow old, our soul will take a toll, for never give up on what you love, for if you grow, you will always be bold, the body may age but your spirit will be connected to your inner soul, for a child will lead them and keep them on the road, it may be narrow at times but Jesus will always comfort you, he will always cleanse your clothes. I am so thankful for my teachers and my classmates, for they have shown me so much love, as the time has went on, I love them all and I hope they never have to experience the blues, or experience any hurt as they are journeying through, for if they need a hand, I will always be there…Even if we are states apart I will stretch my arms as far as I can…I love you all this is my Cosmetology message. P.s. Mrs. Wiggins is the best too, she blessed me my last semester, with two meals a day from the cafe, while I attend school, it feels like Christmas as much as I been blessed, letting these words out, they are coming off my chest! My classmates and teachers have stood the test, I love them so much, this is me confessing after taking these lessons, I'm on a map for success, using my compass, I will lead the rest, a visionary that will pass every test, who loves all people, for we are all of God's beautiful mess…

Chasing inspiration, chasing desperation, taking all these lessons for you are my #1 contestant, I want to be like you, Jesus…You created me before I even could breathe, you spoke me into existence and you gave CPR to me, I gave in to your love for you have loved me, I gave into your trust for you have delivered me, I once was lost but now I see…See it is my past, the reason you are so passionate about me, you took me through storms and tribulation, where I laid on the ground, where I couldn't stop bleeding…I could barely breathe, the rain would fall, the tears would fall, I couldn't bear the weight of my sin it was my final call, Jesus help me!!! Jesus help me!!! God you loved me, God you hunted for me…When I ran from you, you never ran from me…You ran after me…you loved me, and I know I'm not perfect but it is your blood that covers me…I will always be your humble servant, and I will represent the King of Heaven while I'm on Earth, for every person that doesn't know you, I will do everything to influence so they can be birthed again, born again in you God. You will mend the scars, where they are torn apart, it is your amazing love for us that, you are always with us, you will always forgive us, for your son Jesus paid the ultimate price…Thank you God for giving me this life, even through all the pain, it was what I had to go through to impact this generation that is hurting inside, one day you will wipe away every tear that we cried, death will be no more for we will reign with you in the sky, the spirit is writing this, you will always be the light of my life…

As I get lost in your galaxy, as I get lost in your magazine, only ten more minutes till I'm riding in my limousine, as I get lost in the magic scenes, it is then when I really do see, see I'm a poet and I condone it, rising to the top, rising up to my opponent, see he can't see what I see, he doesn't have the vision to plant seeds or chase dreams, that is how you can always see what they can't see…If you want to have the key that unlocks everything, you must be like the hot metal able to mold and do such things, I am a liquid taking the shape of everything I want to be, see as a liquid flows through to the other side so do I, I am walking through doors before I even get inside, I am tackling corps principles before they even can lie, see this system is a rich man's game but I alter my mind so they can't blind me, I long for the night when it is just you and I, listening to the crickets sing as we journey down this path called life, it is in the wilderness where we are free, can you feel that cool breeze, it gives you chills the same kind you give me, for my thoughts created you it is how I created such things, see the creator gave us all the gift to create anything, it is only when you climb the tree, the one only you know how to climb, you see, only then do you awaken the genius inside that the world can't see...Love yourself, identify with your genes, open up to the Holy Spirit let him write your life...I love you Jesus, thank you for rescuing me...

Rock bottom is a beautiful place because you lose it all and realize you never want to lose yourself again...What a phenomenal change happens when we choose to climb than to stay down...God will offer us chances, it is important for us to take them to live the most satisfying life, through becoming better so we can love and serve others... 🙏🙏

Praying Jesus, I just want to be in your presence wrap me in your arms as I do with my blanket, wrap my family in your arms even if it means confessing, we need your holy spirit for guidance to fight these temptations, lead me, Lord...I will chase every dream to reach millions of people to plant every seed...It was through the inspiration of desperation, in my life, that you changed my direction...I love you, Jesus, you keep showering us in your power and protection...Living your vision, it is my confession! Representing the Holy One, my Jesus, for he loves his sons and daughters, we drink upon his water, for we shall never thirst, for his words are worth more than dollars...He is our number one supporter; he's putting this world back in order, rising generations coming after every border…I give the credit of doing hair and literacy to my Heavenly Father ⍰⍰ Poetry by T Harrison

The sky is so blue, the clouds are so gray, the trees are hovering over the water, reflecting on the water, reflecting on the change, the seasons come and go but my love for you will always grow…A cabin in the background is warm as can be, a pile of wood burning outside…in the distance, the grass is so green, where I long for us to meet, where I long for us to greet, for we are never wrong for holding on, see there is power in writing this poem…This is the hour where we belong…The tower of fighting, for rights, for wrongs, showering all of our problems away, loving our self, pursuing our dreams…A couple of lovers, who are kings and queens who find security in taking the lead…Look at the blue eyes, I can see the horizon rise, as I'm swimming in your ocean while eclipsed by your sight…

Okay, sitting out here writing, using both my hands I been climbing, been doing hair since six am, had to pick up the cross at the bridge, searching for the way, for when I hear my name, the crowds go insane, I know I am great, I am overcoming every fear that tried to stop the halt on my peace, see I grin because I am your friend, I been to hell and back that is why I can rhyme with this pen, see the pen has been around since the beginning. Anyone can pick it up but only a special few can let it pick up them. When I am writing, it's my inside spirit coming out, the mind that you are witnessing, the mind that is listening, the mind that is making sense. This mind is my friend, sometimes I don't recognize him for he is different. Not the same person I use to be, oh how proud I am that he has developed into a stylist, a rhymer, a poet that can come out of hiding, let me out, let me shout, these words are coming out of my mouth, these words are more powerful than I can imagine, gasping when I speak to the crowd, have you ever caught your breath after you have been drowning? Have you ever found your crown after getting knocked down? See it started August, let me take it off of pause. 2017 started doing hair, changing people's lives, are they aware? With every action we take, we are affecting the air we operate in, when we choose to be different, we chose to listen to our inner voice, to be truly authentic, we have to let it win, for God designed us from nothing, he made us into something, from dust you see, impacting lives is a must, love and serve, don't give into the corruption, you have to burn the boats, trust your gut, let in the discernment, for the holy spirit lives inside each and every one of us, we are a fragment of Heaven, roaming majestically, this is a must, get your dream and dive for it in the ocean, for the dolphins of life will swim by your side, protecting you from the sharks that try to blind your sight, while acting like your friends in disguise, trust your instinct, have unlimited beliefs, anything can happen, live your dream.

Now that you have made it this far, myself and Lucy create a private organization that houses millions of children that are mistreated, we as partners go out and rescue children from their homes, even creating a time machine where I rescues myself, my brothers, and Lucy, from the home when we were children changing life for eternity…Creating this "Choose Love" foundation that houses millions of kids and adults in a loving environment, where they can choose to leave their home. The children can choose to leave their homes even if the parents don't want to. This organization society can work in, people can learn in, worship in, creating a whole new country for everyone and the only three laws is to love, serve and be good to each other, if they do not abide by these laws, they are kicked out of the foundation while Lucy and I share a romance at the same time while operating the functions of this choose love foundation.

* If they go against the foundation they will be kicked out into the real world which is a dog eat dog world*

"Lucy, come with me, let's go, I know the perfect spot. Let's check out this mysterious cave that rumors the town."

"Okay, Tyler, let's go. I am up for an adventure, I would explore anywhere with you."

Gets in the car and drives to the route.

"Isn't it so amazing how something so simple to us can be so amazing to others, look at the bright yellow stars twinkle in the sky, wouldn't it be incredible flying up that high, experiencing the wind under our wings, soaring over the world as it glimmers in the sky, do you ever wonder if it is just us out there, Tyler?"

"For creation is such a complex beautiful thing, I believe there are creatures of all sorts roaming this galaxy, witnessing what we are going through, true love and happiness, for when I am with you it is just you and I, the world is asleep as you walk by my side, as you talk and it is okay to cry, I cry sometimes too, for we are designed to cry in order to heal, to let the pain leave us through forms of water coming from our wounds. We cry when we are happy too, for something so exciting demands the happiness to flow from our soul. Lucy, we are just about here to the cavern. Follow my lead, turns on the flashlight, forestry surrounds the area as we walk inside the cave."

"This is a little spooky, don't you think, Tyler?"

"Yes, it is but sometimes through overcoming what scares us we can reach the side that is waiting on us."

As we hike through the cave we see all forms of paintings on the wall, forms of electricity painted but from thousands of years ago, we see round flying aircrafts floating in the sky.

"Wow how beautiful, this place is something else, a place I have never experienced before."

We take pictures and continue our walk. I can hear water running.

"Lucy, do you hear that?"

"Yes, look over there, it is a waterfall, how gorgeous."

We walk up to the waterfall, examining the glory it is bestowing upon us, how magnificent…The mist is wetting us down as the water falls into the pool.

"Do you see that, Tyler?"

"See what, Lucy?"

"There is something glimmering behind the falls, let's check it out!"

We walk through the waterfall to realize that there is this room built into the rock on the other side of the falls, inside granite rock. Metal covers the door, opens the door, walking inside this room, all sorts of gadgets associate everywhere in here. *What is this place,* I questioned myself, *am I dreaming?* Whatever had created this device new how to spell, it spelled out travel center on the wall. There was a round gadget, which knowing myself I started playing and fidgeting with, as I turned it the numbers started moving.

"Tyler, I know what this is! This is a time machine, this will allow us to travel back in time…"

"Whoa, Lucy. I always wanted to be rescued when I was a child. Now I have that power in the palm of my hands."

"I wanted to be rescued as a child too, Tyler. What do you say?"

"Let's go, rescue ourselves before the hate began, what do you say, Lucy?"

"Let's do it, we will travel to the year 2000, rescue ourselves, come back to the machine and come back to this time. Before we go, come here…"

Hugs Lucy, kisses Lucy, and embraces the moment.

"Okay let's go."

Turns the knob to 2000, presses green for travels, you would think the room would shake, but it doesn't but something else does happen, we can feel the electricity flowing through our body as we travel through. I rescued myself when I was four before myself or my brothers were messed with by my cousin or experienced any more physical or verbal abuse by our father, we then proceeded to go get Lucy. After we gathered each other, we headed back to the travel center.

"Lucy let's create a world full of goodness when we get back to 2018, a world that we govern, but it isn't a rule-based government or a tax-based government, it isn't even a government at all but an atmosphere full of happiness, love and peace. We will go out and rescue thousands of children that will be our mission, while housing millions of adults and children, who choose to be a representation of who we were created to be. A reflection of Heaven, a reflection of God's kingdom, for he loves us and we will love them, the only rules for it will be that you have to choose love, happiness, and service to others in order to experience complete freedom. If you go against it, you will be kicked out into the dog eat dog world. What do you say, Lucy?"

"That is my calling of course, I am in, I want to rescue others from others, and from themselves." We arrive back in 2018 with four children with us this time, kind of can't fathom that we just time travelled, also rescuing ourselves from our past.

"This is such a beautiful existence, what a marvelous world it is out there and we haven't even scratched the surface, well almost ha-ha."

"Tyler you are such a goof, I am so glad I found you, for I will always be with you, I will always listen to you, I love you, you have changed my perspective, changed the way I look at life, you are my one and only, I would love to spend this life by your side."

Tyler gets on one knee, "Would you marry me Lucy?"

"Yes, found true love to be true, found that you always find the answers when you are telling the truth, if you buy into the news the government feeds us, you will always be a fool. That is why we don't watch the news. We will start building our organization tomorrow and we will post flyers up so we can search for participants who want to be a part of this world. We will build, we will love, we will restore, and we will serve, liberating the world as we know it."

"I love you, Lucy. I am so glad I found you."

"Writing a book is an adventure. To begin with it is a toy and an amusement. Then it becomes a mistress, then it becomes a master, then it becomes a tyrant. The last phase is that just as you are about to be reconciled to your servitude, you kill the monster and fling him to the public."

– Winston Churchill

I love you all, thank you for reading, love others, be good to others, develop yourself so you can love and serve more. Keep your eyes open and aware of where you are headed! This story of how I overcame the odds! I pray that my poetry has sparked the creativity in you all, that you truly appreciate the art as much as I do. My second novel will be titled Lucy, I Found Her, and I am going to Marry Her. The second novel I will really delve into the storyline.

She ran after Ed Sheeran, she tanned with Ed Sheeran, she made plans with this music man, that later developed into a live romance, he took her by the hand, he touched her skin, what started off as friends became more as these lovers danced, she looked him in the eyes, it took him by surprise, she was crying, not from hurt but from the joy she was hiding, he laughed, she sighed, perfect duet played very quietly, as the sunset raised, this new sound love had bitten both of them, by the end of the night. Spending the day together, dancing in the rain together, changing scenery, witnessing all sorts of weather, letting the soul roam as I write this letter, the story of how Ed Sheeran and his wife, were led by each other.

That's the slogan, ain't it? NF on the mic, rapping for his rights, banging on the walls, he started painting pictures with his words, now they are all hanging, twisted with his verse, he got crowds shaking, dressed in all black...

Not even the curse of the black pearl can replace him!

This lack of words may prevent me from having her, this lack of verbs may prevent me from capturing her, this passing verse is something that I'm after...even if she doesn't choose me, I can still make it without her...Just thankful I had the moments to share, getting to encounter her...May life give us everything, we are after...For when time turns the page, we will start our new chapter...

It is in the night that the lights come alive, it is by your side that the darkness does decline, it is in our sight, what we feel comes to life, it is the coolness of the air that covers our mind...

I believe this book is bigger than me if I'm being honest...This is more than just a contest but a conquest as an artist...Lucy, I Couldn't Find Her So I Created Her

See the clouds are often white, it's in the crowds that I find my mind. It's about the time that I reveal what's been inside. It is this creative spirit that has come out of hiding...Manifest what you believe, dive through the air as you spread your wings. ▯

First time visiting England, I realized that there weren't many penguins, of all the shenanigans, the birds were flying, this place called England was vividly-colored, the color of autumn dawned upon the lawn, the colors of October was a blanket upon our hearts, the way people laughed and smiled had me mesmerized, wow...Beautiful people, wonderful places, and the way they chased when they saw my face...England freedom, the government cares for the people, holding the crown, holding the town, showing my girlfriend around, the way the cobbled road turns, the sound of horses galloping around, in awe of this breathtaking fountain, this is where we first met, this is where we first left the past behind, this is where we closed our eyes, two friends who were lovers in disguise, our hearts were warmed, every ounce was a cry

When you die you are skydiving in the opposite direction towards the heavens as your spirit connects to the universe.

I really can't believe this is happening...Can't believe I made it, I didn't write to get famous...I write to impact generations of people...Getting paid and becoming Famous was just a part of it...

Collection of poetry while maintaining a storyline as I wrestle and grapple with difficult concepts in an abstract creative way.

By writing my book I captured history while creating the future all at the same time...♥

I couldn't find her so I created her, I couldn't deny her so I dated her, my thoughts were puzzled, what was I doing here? Listen, everyone, this love is for all the noise...This choice was for all the choices...Connecting to my inner child is something that I got to do. In order to step into my imagination, to fight the dark with the light, my dude...I had to step into the solitude, calling on his promises too, see he planted his light in you...I couldn't find her so I created her, grappling with new concepts, I got them from downstairs, see these emotions are powerful, us as humans are unstoppable, see we create with thoughts, we partake in this walk, we write our names with chalk, just so they can wash us away, treating us like we are nothing at all...Love is the cause, serving is greatest of all. Love your soul, Love the cross...

Been climbing through a tunnel ever since I been underground, I broke through to the surface, now my name is talked about in every town! One love for all, one by one and all for all.

I've got the words to change these places, I've got the answers to all these questions, by examining our spirits can we truly make exchanges, of who we are and who we are in desperation. Of anything that changes we are here to make the changes, writing what is real is the only way to understand these cages...

Everyone is so scared to let God possess their spirit because they think they will be missing out on life...Truth is if you don't give in to the Holy Spirit who created you, you are missing out...

Fiction is real for those that live there...

I Found Her and I'm About to Marry Her

Blue skies reflected off the water, very few clouds we witnessed with our eyes, a small kingdom that was surrounded by water and forestry. Colors of green encompassed this area of existence. This architecture was something I had never experienced, the structure captivated every inch of my being. There she was, dressed in all white when she looked me in the eyes, time stopped, my heart was thumping, my tears started flowing, as a dove lands on a branch, she appeared out of nowhere and landed upon my heart. She was riding in a carriage pulled by horses, as she stepped out, I held her hand while she held my mind.

"Tyler, look at you, you are breaking down from the emotions you are expressing, but I will build you up and love and comfort you." This wasn't a traditional wedding with bridesmaids and best men, but the auditorium filled up with people. Voices of angelic sounds emitting, filled the presence giving us chills. The priest waited for us by the cross in front of the congregation, I walked her down the aisle as she walked with me throughout my life. We stood there bestowing each other's love for one another, painting this picture with words, she inspired a love that I had never known. It was the time, the crowds got quiet, the singing stopped, it was time to say our vows.

"I, Tyler, take thee, Lucy, to be my wedded husband/wife, to have and to hold, from this day forward, for better, for worse, for richer, for poorer, in sickness and in health, to love and to cherish, till death do us part, according to God's holy ordinance; and thereto I pledge thee my faith [or] pledge myself to you."

"I do," replied Lucy.

"I do," replied myself.

"You may kiss the bride," replied the priest.

At that moment, it was a communion of our two souls becoming intertwined. We were two entities before we got married now we represented one in the spiritual sense, she was still there in the physical, our souls were one now, everything she was had been added unto me, and everything I was had been added unto her. Tears of joy filled the church, it was her and I now, and we walked hand in hand down the aisle, exiting the church. The horse and carriage awaited us.

"Where to?" asked the coachman.

"Take us to the castle where we reside."

We both climbed into the carriage. We immediately were drawn to each other, we wrapped each other in arms, kissing slowly yet intimately at the same time. I ran my fingers through her hair, she ran her hands up my chest, her lips caressed mine, we were breathing heavily from all the love that was flowing from our chest, we stayed dressed but we were so infatuated, with each other that we didn't hold back.

The coach slowed down, the coachman announced, "Hey, you two love birds, we have arrived at our destination."

The castle awaited us, waiting on us as we have waited for it, I picked her up and carried her in my arms, walking through the entrance, and our butler opened the gate for us to enter. I carried her up the stairwell, our castle had the aroma of vanilla, it was intricately designed, a living space for Kings and his Queens.

"Tyler, I love you so much, thank you for loving me when I couldn't love myself. Thank you for holding me when I couldn't hold my own hand. Thank you for showing me how a man is supposed to treat a woman. Most of all, thank you for rescuing me, for even, through the tests you fortified all of the truths."

"Lucy...You were the one that saved me...I will always love you..."

I carried her to the bedroom, laying her down, climbing on top of her, kissing her lips as our spirits connected. I sucked on her neck, kissing down it, pulling her dress off, unfastening her bra, then she proceeded to take my clothes off. We made love, our flesh was becoming one, our love was growing even stronger, our connection was getting even taller, and our commitment was the best decision of all. Memories like this have changed our life, centuries like this have caused us to glide. We shared our love for each other in bodily form. We unleashed everything we were into each other, when we were finished we held each other, securing each other, protecting each other, caring for each other, romancing each other, for those that don't believe in that fairy-tale love have never experienced it, only those who can comprehend and digest what it means to love someone, through the good times and the bad times will know the definition of what true love is.

"I love you, Tyler. I am about to fall asleep, I will see your beautiful face when I wake in the morning."

"I love you too, Lucy, goodnight darling."

The room had an aura, it had peace, and it had a heavenly-being that watched over us. Our guardian angels were there to make sure we slept soundly with no interruptions from the demons. The stars looked very different tonight, as our love aligned so did the stars, you could hear the heaven's divinity pour out on us, as the serenity freed us from our captivity. Something happened that day, the unseen had never tasted, or could they imagine, what it meant as these two love birds were met with compassion. From the ashes we rose, through the patches, we were made whole, though we were cut, we were healed spiritually from inside our soul. This passage was frozen, our actions were golden, and the passion that was chosen was a mixture of what has been unspoken. The tokens of love, gratitude surpassed all of the commotion of what it meant to be truly awakened, not being blinded by our sight, not being cut with this knife, instead using water to cleanse our eyes, removing the paint that the system has painted over our eyes, being enlightened is a special thing, everyone can connect to the world if they believe such things. You have to connect to it if you want to see what I see, you have to take the earplugs out, in order to hear these voices that talk to me, and they are from the spiritual world. Throw away your fears and doubts, truly believing, the most beautiful things are right before your eyes, as you read each word as it comes alive, holding this work in your hands, can you finally understand the information I am presenting and I am not from this land. My Heavenly Father represents the kingdom at hand, I am just the vessel allowing him to type with my hands. This is a message for the whole world to comprehend, see my Father just wants a relationship with you, not a bunch of rules and regulations that the men have come up with. If just one person could fathom the topics I am discussing, if just one nation would show love for all humanity, recognizing their savior then my mission would be complete. I sent Jesus to suffer for you all that is how much love I have for the cross. I am not distant and angry, please stop making each other hate me, and I will be here for you even when you can't take me. To end all suffering, it is my desire that you may love, comfort, and help one another. See we create with thoughts, we love with our heart, we discern with our stomach it is the art. I designed you all like that...I operate in the ways that you do, but sin has corrupted your flesh causing you to go against who and what I created for you. The devil may walk this earth, but so do I, the time will come when I will call for the ones that believe in me and we shall descend into the sky. We shall descend with a trumpet on high as the holy one washes away every sin while wiping away every cry. The Devil and I shall have a toe to toe fight for I will cast all his demons and himself in the lake of fire. Death shall be no more, no more hurting or evil will roam these heavens I created, the temple lives on the inside, you must knock on the door. Knock and I shall answer, ask and you shall receive if it means you are hurting or helping, show love to those in need, these keys, these dreams, I have the utmost faith in humanity, we must get back to representing the king. Why do you all kill one another, I killed my son Jesus to take on the suffering of the world, wasn't that enough? He rose after three days to show that I am for you not against you. Forgive them, Father, they know not what they do, they kill, hate, and destroy each other allowing the demons to toxify their spirit, are they even aware that they are possessed, puppets that work for the devil, that bastard is going to pay and I promise it will be soon. I love all my little children that I created, why did you turn on me Lucifer? I made you one of the most beautiful angels, I gave you the gifts to create music, you gave into the wickedness, the greed, the selfishness, wanting my role as creator, turning your back on me, you signed up for a death wish, you should know that it won't be long till I destroy you and the angels that followed you. I shall create a new heaven and a new earth, you will never have the opportunity to join my loved ones on these streets of gold. You shall burn in another dimension for eternity, along with all your followers, there will be no one to save you, you made your choices and now you have to follow through. I gave you the most beautiful voice now the only sounds you will compose are screams as the pain consumes you. To all my little children I love all of you, don't forget about me and I won't forget about you, who knows when I will come, it may be tomorrow, or it may be this afternoon, for no one knows except me and when I do come back, you will all know it too. The clouds shall open up, the blood of Jesus shall fill a full moon, a trumpet will sound, for this, I have written every word is truth, just like I inspired men to write the bible, I am inspiring Tyler to write what I have assigned for him to write, this is your beacon of hope, this is your season of growth, this is the reason for all of the lost ones that do not know, that I came to save the world, not to condemn the world, I came to change the world not destroy the world, I came so that you may gain my love because I love you. I'm still here Tyler, fear not for I have been with you through all you're suffering, I shall use you to represent my kingdom saving these lost souls. The sunshine entered into the window, red and blue cardinals flew in flying around the both of us, beautiful sounds entered into the bedroom, you could hear the piano play but there wasn't a piano, you could hear the choirs singing but there wasn't any choirs present, what was present was two angels standing guard, protecting us as we slept. We knew they were there all alone so we weren't startled much.

"We have a message for you two, the kingdoms rejoiced yesterday as you all were joined in Holy Matrimony, your Heavenly Father wept at the first sign knowing that you had found her, now you all are reconciled as one, as we are reconciled as one with our Heavenly Father. We have special plans for you and Lucy, we are sending you all to a special world for your honeymoon if you all will please come this way."

Lucy and I both got out of bed, we showered together, and I washed her body as she washed mine. We got dressed, we grabbed our suitcases, packed the essentials: toothbrushes, toothpaste, shirts, shoes, phones, chargers, personal hygiene items.

"Are you ready for this babe?"

"As always, I would go anywhere as long as you are by my side darling."

The voyage awaits, everything was packed, and we brought everything with us that was essential including our belief because if we didn't believe none of this would be happening.

"Are you all ready?" asked the angels

"Yes," we replied, "we are ready to start this journey."

We gathered in a circle, the angels grabbed both of our hands, we closed our eyes, all in unison we said, "Praise the Holy One, Praise the Lord on High."

In the blink of an eye, we were in this majestic place. We arrived next to a beautiful stream of water. Hundreds of creatures surrounded us playing flutes, violins, and harps. These creatures ranged from lions, tigers, lizards, talked in our language and responded the way we responded. Your highness the king waits for you, and your wife, we have special plans for the love that you both are experiencing. They gathered our belongings loaded them on the boat, we boarded the boat and we proceeded up the river. The colors of the leaves were red and white, representing the blood of Jesus. The white was the purity of his love for us, how he washes us white as snow, this wasn't heaven but every world recognized the creator. Every animal recognized the savior, every being testified the truth sounding off in unison as they read these words off the pages. Hundreds of dolphins swam about the boat, jumping out the water, speaking in their language, what a breathtaking moment to soak in, how in the world did we get so lucky to experience all of this love, joy, and happiness? Lucy and I held hands as we stood on the front of the boat, I kissed her lips, thank you, God, for blessing us in this manner. Thank you, Dad, for choosing Lucy and me when you planned creation, thank you for being an infinite God giving us the power to create as you created this world, allowing us to make these changes. See he gave me the talent to write these pages, the system of education set me up to fail, I was never created to do Algebra, I was never created to be a scientist, God created me to be a writer, to be an instrument for him as I influence millions of people. Education is a good thing because it shows us what we are good and bad at, we shouldn't be penalized for not having the ability to learn certain material. We all have different capabilities. Learning is a great thing, but trying to push us all through the same mold, like pushing cattle from one area to another, is causing people to believe they are idiots when we are all intelligent creatures. We all have different gifts, talents, and abilities, don't let the system of education program you to hate learning just because they want to treat you like a robot. We are not robots but we are wonderfully and fearfully made. Everything we need is inside of us when you truly awaken, you will realize this prophecy that you are witnessing, you will have a shift in your thinking and yes people may think you are crazy, but after a while, they will be the crazy ones for not believing. It is my mission to open people's eyes for the rest of my life. As long as there's breath in my lungs, I shall use the skills God provided me with to be an influential member of society. I will travel this world representing love and happiness. Yes, they may persecute me but I will always stand firm in what I have seen and what I haven't seen, please whatever you do. Please love yourself, please love others, please be good to others, please sacrifice for others, and please be there for all of your brothers and sisters. May your mind be opened after you read my material, may you cross every ocean as you step into the temple, may you be conscious of the spirit that lives inside of you, may you always breathe new life every moment, defeating all of the evil for you shall conquer every dark night with the light from the moon, may you read these novels multiple times so you can get the picture I am painting too. Representing the real news, the options that follow this solitude has allowed me to keep pouring abstract creativity for every lightning strike, boom! This is my power place, this literary analysis can't be replaced, the words are powerful, the verbs are a mouthful, may you outrun the chase of the enemy for when he comes after you, don't give in to the doubts or fears my dude. Call on your creator for he loves you too.

"Do you see that, Lucy?"

"What is it, Tyler, those mountains ahead?"

"Yes, babe but they are covered in symbols, symbols representing love, happiness, and gratitude. These are the most important symbols representing who our spirits long to be, the love is expressed as the eagle, as it soars through the air coming from the heavens stunning seas, it captures glimpses of aerial views, it breathes life into the ashes too, it contains the symbolism of his holy presence, and what he will want us to do. The Lions of the past are here too, smiling from ear to ear, showing true happiness for it is advanced as us in spirit, still chooses joy, it still chooses to reveal all the blissfulness of gratitude, king of God's jungle, roaming while navigating for it walks with my Uncle, a warrior on this island, but these Lions will not bite a single man, these creatures represent peace and happiness. Finally, dwarf kittens representing the power of love, Mother Earth is a spiritual realm, so many people think we are physical beings trying to understand the spiritual world. In reality, we are spiritual beings who have been brainwashed believing the physical is all there is. We are spiritual beings trying to understand this physical world that my Father created for us."

"Tyler, we are arriving, look there, thousands of these creatures, I mentioned, were at the top of this mountain as the rowers rowed us up the stream."

Angelic angel voices traveled from up ahead, radiating off of the water, something mysterious was happening to Lucy and I as we arrived, we began to echo in this language we had never known, reality began to shift as we were coming close to the entrance, rainbows filled the skies as Mother Earth started to breathe her life, she made movements, the ground shifted, the trees were reckless in their pursuit as the gates opened as we rowed on in through.

"We have been waiting for you King Tyler and Queen Lucy, we have been watching over you since the day God chose to put you two here. We represent love for we are not from here, we come from above, the pain you experienced when you were young, and you will have no remembrance of it after I place my hand on your third eye, releasing all of the sufferings that you two have known. You will still have the memories but you will be numb from the hurt, for he sent you all to suffer so he can represent love. Every good gift comes from his hand, he comes to demonstrate through hardships that he is still alive and still using humans to come out of hiding, while speaking in their language, letting the words flow, for the movement of water has a direction, as he moves your tongue."

We got off of the boat; the lions, tigers, lizards, all assisted in helping us get our goods off of the boat, everyone surrounded us, hugging us, holding us, lifting us up overhead the crowds.

"Bring them to me we heard in a loud harmonic sound."

"Yes master," the crowds replied.

Lucy and I were both being carried, everyone in the room cried out, "Hail the Holy Ones, Hail the Holy Ones, Hail the Holy Ones."

"My name is Paul, I am one of Christ's disciples, I have walked this Earth for 2000 years, I have walked next to Jesus recording all of his wonderful works, I was even there to witness his birth, I was there when God created Adam and Eve creating these creatures from dirt, I have been here all along with every being that has walked this Earth. I am at a loss of words though, Jesus came to demonstrate that he is for us not against us. Why must so many people give in to the Devil's work? Why can't they choose to represent Christ as you two have, I have chosen you, Tyler to bring my kingdom down to Earth, you make your daddy proud, yay though at times you doubted him as Peter has, you still chose to walk on water, putting your faith in him through the storms and the troubles, through the hardships and the pain, you have loved everyone you came into contact with, little do you know you are representing me. I am glad you made it, I am glad you poured your story out on this paper, I am sad about all the hurt that took place in the matter, just know that you will no longer hurt, that glass that you hold shall no longer be shattered. As I have written, you must have the faith to call forth the things that are not as if they were, you listened to me when you read the verses, you hearkened to me, and time after time I spoke to you from this spiritual world. You cooperated with the mission Jesus placed you on. God and his angels rejoice as we rejoice, as you gave into the spiritual world, for if you walk after the flesh you will die, but if you walk after the one that created the flesh you shall live."

"What's the matter, Lucy," I asked her.

"Tyler, it is finished. The hurt we have is over now. The prophecy proves we are chosen now. The angels sound off with trumpets sound as we liberate the world while we love each other through every sound."

"I wrap her in my arms and kiss her, I hold her face with my hands as we both wept here, for we are no longer asleep, we are no longer held in captivity getting defeated, we are no longer a slave to these people, we are no longer a drain, that gets beaten by the evil, we are children of God we are his kingdom."

Paul speaking, "Our Father writes, it is written; it is not good for man to be alone. I have aligned you Tyler to compose the most beautiful poems, I have aligned you, Lucy, to be his backbone, for when you two are together you are most powerful, the intelligence I have given the both of you is incomprehensible, the agenda I have placed on you two, if you do not know it now, which I am sure you do, all your days are numbered in my book for I know the thoughts I have designated for you too. This is all finally starting to make sense, Lucy, the puzzle pieces are all starting to fit, the spaces are starting to be filled, and connecting the dots is becoming so real. From the feelings you feel, from the emotions you have spilled, from the heartbreak that has broken many, it's a hard pill to swallow.

The hurt that we went through made us so hollow but it is his Holy Presence that came inside, mending all that the demons came to borrow, healing us from the inside, for the enemy will no longer be able to touch you, for you are my sons and my daughters, you, after all, have hope for tomorrow, for I love you both and will take away every sorrow. It is my desire to give you everything you want, but you must ask with a heart to help, not a heart to hurt, you must receive these blessings from this spiritual realm, as you represent my kingdom as you walk this earth. Here lately I been fasting, here lately I been reacting to the Holy Spirit, he is more than atoms, he is a protractor on a map helping us coordinate where he wants us to go, preventing us from entering a disaster, preventing us from getting crushed by these actors, restoring our soul, restoring our shows, breathing new light into these lost souls, be conscious of who you are and what is about to unfold. Truth be told, his love covers us all, you can persecute him, you can beat him, you can forget about him, but when it is you that is taking the beaten, he will pick you up and mend your soul. He will touch your skin with his hands, healing what was broke, he is a God of miracles he loves us all. He will take away the 20 years of pain as you journeyed down this road, as a lost cause, give in to the Holy Spirit, believe me, it may be hard to bestow, the regret that can haunt us when we are old, we are closer to meeting him face to face as our spirit detaches from our bones."

The creatures began to play instruments in the background.

"Now all that is out of the way follow me this way," Paul said aloud.

137

This living area inside this cavern was breathtaking, crystals and granite filled the walls, gemstones of all sorts were everywhere, they released energy into the world, they represented healing for the soul. Smooth diamonds are what we walked on, all the floors were from diamonds, there was honey for everyone, and these bees won't sting you but kiss you instead. Every being here was the compounds of love including the insects.

"This honey is different, it is sealing all of our wounds from the external world, and the rejuvenation was a declaration of the balance of Lucy and me becoming one."

We walked into this lively auditorium where a table about 200-feet long by six-feet wide held the most delicious delicacies, Lucy and I were starving. Paul made a special announcement to all of the creatures as we all sat down to eat.

"If you would please join me in the celebration of our Kings and Queens who have suffered long enough, they shall know suffering no more, I encourage you all to make them welcome here, showing them at home as they are newlyweds, they will need some privacy together, my tour guides shall set up events every day for you all to journey outside exploring the specific location we are at and the beautiful environment that surrounds us all. With that being said, let us feast! Let us drink, let us be merry as we dance with our feet, let us be excited expressing our dreams, into the east, into the west, instruments play, people are at rest, I am proud of you Lucy and Tyler, you both are the best, you both are majestic spirits, as the colors radiate from your chest, auras radiate from our heads, you both are instantly healed for I cleanse you both in the Holy Ghost, we drink upon this wine as we eat upon this bread, in communion with our Lord God, he has always had the best interest in where we go."

"Lucy, gosh you are really beautiful, the way your hand holds mine has me longing for your hand until the end of time, the way you hold me when I'm all tired and ready for bed, it has me longing to hold you for the rest of my life."

Our eyes are the windows to our spirit, our ears are the windows that we listen with, our hands are the instruments that allow us to present what we are thinking, as I press these buttons while making sense, these letters on the keyboard are all individual but when I put them together it creates a masterpiece, I don't know how I do this but the spirit knows how to present this information if you are looking for how-to, I will tell you to search within for everything you need already lives inside of you, the creator gave us all the ability to create with every action that we do, we can choose it in love, we can choose it as an out too, for these legs allow us to roam, these legs allow us to travel, explore while we are entering the zone as I pick up this phone, dialing these numbers, what do these numbers mean? Symbols that I press that allow me to reach the ones in need, if you want to live the most satisfying life rule number one, never give up on your dreams, never neglect yourself casting down who you were created to be, call on the holy one whether you are on the mountain top or whether you are in the valley screaming for help in your time of need, it's in these caverns that I go it's in these passages that no one knows I am moving through these thoughts in my head, I am channeling information, death is a lie, for no one shall die, your flesh may deteriorate but this spirit that I give you shall reign with me in the sky. Fly high with me, ride your bike with me, climb the signs with me, light up your lighter with me, casting out all darkness opening the door to the light as we spread our wings. It is an attitude to operate in the altitudes don't be afraid of your belief system, for there is power in your existence, there is a survivor in all of you, there's a reason my goal is 2,000-words a day writing for all of you. Go ahead examine me with your thoughts, take notes as your jaw drops as you wonder, how I string these words together as you follow along. As a spider composes her web, I let these words come straight from inside my head, as a dog barks when someone needs help, I shall carry the torch for everyone that needs the help, I will take up for all the ones hurting, for I know pain but I have been delivered by these thoughts in my brain. Forgive me if these concepts are hard to understand it is my mission to end suffering for everyone, it is what I represent, music is healing these thoughts have been giving birth since the beginning, my heart will always have a love for winning, for it is more than just a win, I am more than just your friend, if you ever need someone to call, go right ahead it maybe three in the morning but I will answer it, it may be the moment before you give into the selfishness that I will lend a hand, please never kill yourself, God will take your story, restore your soul, cleanse you from the inside out, that is just the way that he rolls, rolling with punches, jumping with the lunges, plunging through the system, now I have all of the tongues listening. I have all the songs glistening, I am not a God but I do represent the king, it is his majesty dressed in all purple, he came for me at the graveyard, dug me from the dirt as he ruffled through the earth, as he wrestled with this shovel as he saved me on this earth. Why I still can't find the words to describe why he would rescue me, it was only my desires to be loved while loving everything, to trust but the ones I trusted end up hurting me, the ones that we're supposed to take care of me ripped my childhood away, because of that, that is how I can write such things, please end the suffering, please stop the hurting, for there may come a time when everyone will destroy everything, giving in to the corruption, everyone will die, everyone will lose their life, all because people chose, hate instead of life, that is why I am so passionate about the love that comes from above, please love yourself please love others, please. Our whole world will never be the same again, if we choose to walk in the direction of love, we must choose to walk in happiness for it is God's way to account for these sins. He covers us, he loves us, he will always be our best friend, for he is here in the good times and he is here as we coast with this wind, this life is a roller coaster my friend, full of ups and downs, full of phenomenal events, full of tragedies for those that have truly been hurt can latch their soul to a pen, allowing their mind to become one with the ink, if I was to have a drink, I prefer half and half sweet tea, the flavor is so delicious. As I drop this rock in the water, the ripples flow from one side to the other, as I pour this water on the rock, the rock stays in the same place in the same concept as you read this material, I am creating waves that vibrate in your mind, I am changing the tune, this story was written to change all of you, letting go of the hate and letting in the love. It is her and I, it is her and I all of the time, it is her that reaches for my eyes when she turns off the light, it is her that fights for me when I am too tired to fight, it is her light that kisses me when I close my blinds, it is in her sight that she loves me and I love her for she is my wife, she is my life, she is my ride or die, she's the one I dream about every night, knowing that I get to wake up every morning, looking her in her beautiful eyes. This magic that she and I have matched, she holds me in her arms, she always has the pass, she always knows what comes first and what comes last, she takes care of me and I provide for her at last. After we all feasted Paul showed us to our room, we both laid down stuffed full of drinks and food. What a time to be alive, what a time to be able to write, oh how I love my darling, oh how I love my wife.

"I love you, baby."

"I love you too, Tyler."

Until we rise in the morning goodnight. Gets underneath the covers cuddling as we fall asleep in the dead of night, oh how brightly the stars twinkle for they light up our lives. I was having a very vivid dream tonight. I was in this city looking for my Lucy and I couldn't find her. I went from shop to shop looking for her. I went from top to bottom, frantically asking townspeople about her. I sent out multiple missing signs for her. Even though she was by my side, in my dream she was missing. It was real for me for my dreams are real for me.

I end up knocking on the Mayor's house.

"Have you seen my dear Lucy?"

"No sir, I haven't but there was a man in a black cloak wandering through town, it made me put up my suspicions, so I put a word throughout town that everyone stays inside during daylight hours." Hmm, that is weird and very suspicious, after searching throughout the town, there was only one spot left to check, it was her favorite spot to be, the waterfall of many colors, colors of the rainbow emitted from this wonderful work created by God. Representing I shall never flood the earth again, for when the time comes I will call my followers home, I shall shut down this third dimension, destroying the earth with fire and brimstone, creating the new heavens and earth which shall be the fourth dimension.

I ran through the city, screaming, "Lucy! Lucy! Where are you?!" I ran from the city, down this nature trail, that was full of ups and downs from the terrain. I was running towards the falls. As I approached, there was a darkness that covered the falls.

"Jesus! Jesus!" I called on my Heavenly Father to fight this spiritual battle for me.

"Do not be afraid child, this nuisance that works for the devil shall suffer in the lake of fire, and not one single demon shall come against my children and get away with it. For the demons tremble at the sound of my name, the evil shakes, for they know I am the temple, for I once loved them but they chose differently. Lucifer your follower chose to suffer for eternity as you have, now I shall cast him into the lake of fire, this is a warning for you, for your time shall come when I cast you out of existence for all of eternity. Be gone you waste of an angel, you chose the darkness, choosing to walk away from the one who created creation."

The waterfall was restored to its beauty, as Lucy screamed my name, "Tyler! Tyler! Tyler! Is that you?"

Yes, my love, I have come for you, I called on our Heavenly Father and he rescued us from the monster."
Hugs and kisses each other

"I couldn't find you, love, I searched everywhere for you, I talked to the mayor, I talked to the townspeople, there was only one spot left I knew to check and that was here, you will always be the missing piece, when I am away from you, for no matter what happens I will always come after you, I don't care if it costs me everything as long as you are okay." *breathing heavily*

"I love you, Tyler. You are the love of my life, you are the missing song I search for, the one that I play over and over again, for the thoughts of you always encompass my mind, as a shepherd carries a lamb, our Father carries us close to our heart, as people search for food, he shall break the bread feeding all of the ones who are suffering from the torment of the demons, our God will always come through. As the cold of night approaches he will provide sheltering too, every good gift comes from his hand, isn't it so incredible how he can take care of millions of people all at the same time, simultaneously for his love is greater than the moon." *Wraps Lucy in my arms.*

The morning was here, I woke up and there she was, sleeping beauty, breathing so beautifully, her inhale and exhale affected my mood causing me to fall deeper in love as I examined her while we slept in this gorgeous room. I kissed her cheeks.

She replied, "Good morning love, will you please rub my feet, all those travels yesterday caused some soreness."

"Yes, darling." I grabbed some warming lotion, brought the chair to the edge of the bed as I touched her skin, using petrissage, effleurage, friction, and tapotement massage techniques.

"Baby that feels amazing, how on earth did I find you? How on earth did you find me? I believe God allowed our spirits to connect, we were always apart of each other's destiny. We were created to cross the winds, the trials, the hard experiences, they have helped shape you and me. What do you want to do today?"

I overheard Paul saying that he has unicorns in the stable that we could ride together along the crystal sea. That sounds alluring, I am already lured in, let us do that my dear. We both took a bath together, this bathroom was glorious, gemstones, crystals, diamonds, obsidian were in the walls and floor, the sinks were made of stone, the bath and shower held a stream that always flowed from above in the cavern, it was the perfect temperature too. The bath was very roomy, but we wanted to be close as lovers are, so we were all over each other tending to each other as we cleansed each other in this hot spring. Her hair had this shine, the way the colors radiated when I shampooed it, the colors were so bright, and I could see them even when I close my eyes.

"Lucy when we get dressed before we go on our adventure, I am going to put two Dutch braids in your hair, Dutch braids are very pretty braids." She washed my hair, washed my back, we fully washed each other, and no we didn't have a heart attack. The healthy abundant love that we shared was surreal. No one could break this connection, no one could change our direction, no one could ask a wrong question, for when she is with me, and we will always get to our destination. If you are looking for an explanation of how this happened, if you are searching for the dedication to read the next chapter, just remember one word at a time, one word holds so much passion, these

145

words are bigger than I, there is a breathtaking kingdom that reigns in the sky. The kingdom holds all the answers, the kingdom holds every cry. This was the most authentic living, I have every digested, this was the most complex yet simple visions that I have witnessed, this was more than a moment, this was a lifelong decision, sharing it with the love of my life, boy does she know how to cook in the kitchen. Knowing that wherever I go, I shall come back to her by the end of the night, she comforts me with her food as she holds my soul tight. Takes care of me, I take care of her for she is the perfect wife. This journey has been emotional, it has been a roller coaster coasting on this ship as we crossed different oceans in our life, and it has been a commotion as the waves beat upon the rocks why do they cry? For even the rocks shall praise his name for he is the lord of all time, he controls every moment, he controls every rhyme, he is the lord most high for we worship him always, he always holds our minds. There she was levitating on a cloud, the cloud has stars in it, they cover her all around, there she is wearing her crown, as the lights light up from the back, she is wearing the most amazing crafted gown, galaxies of stars are in the background, even the place called mars is on track now, a thick abstract red line splits these two realities, colors of blue encircle this imagery, substances of growth capture what is missing, there is still hope for humanity, there is still hope for all of these children. See this book is more than just hooking the reader, these sentences are more than just capturing the creator, the paragraphs are more than the these missing craters, the pages in this book may be thin but the descriptions will cause a shift in the wind, causing all of the world to be awakened to my best friend.

Her name is Lucy, she is a cutie, she has a cute little booty for I oftentimes catch myself admiring her beauty, I oftentimes feel like she and I are in a movie that I directed, I never mind getting her cuddles, for she is my lover and she is amusing. She has this special feature about her, she can discern without knowing, she can create without composing, she can manipulate these words out of nothing, oh the talent we both have, oh how she is the most beautiful person. She has the most creative purses, she has the most creative verses, she makes the most innovative commotions for when she is with me she is the potion, and she heals me as I heal all of her emotions. Oh how peaceful, oh how she is never deceitful, oh how she captures all time, when she and I are together, no account of evil shall come between this divine appointment, created by God. She is the keyhole, I am the key, for we both are information, for we both unlock our dreams, for we see what they can't see, we see the invisible what most people can't see, we are all from another world, how many words do I have to write for you all to get that we are creative human beings? We are in theaters with a lot of people, we are the main source of conversation, and we are the points that point out, as you point out what you see. These metaphors are for than metal floors, these similes hold more power than you and me can adore, this exoskeleton, this being, I am oh so thankful, God thought of us when he chose to give us these gifts, to set you all free from the captivity. These letters are more than just letters, yeah they may make up words, and they also create headers. A lighthouse that is at bay for when I search, my spirit is searching for the right words to say. I search these messages for more than what they mean, only then can I truly awake to this information as I am planting all of these seeds. Time does not matter when I am writing, it is in the morning that I am most creative, I arise with the sun, I take a shower, drink some coffee, put on some relaxing music as I step into the other side when my fingers touch the keyboard, these stories flow from the inside, the blessings are blessed, the gratitude we express has us longing for every breath, for I am thankful for all of the trials and tribulations that arise with each new test, yes it may be difficult sometimes but our Heavenly Father always allows us to rest. Thank you, Jesus you are the best, thank you for my wife, thank you for bringing us out of that mess, thank you for all of creation, thank you for the sky. We both had finished showering, we both got dressed in outfits composed of flowers, and it won't be long till we are riding these extravagant creatures. *Kisses Lucy*

"Are you ready for this adventure my love?"

"Yes, my darling, I can't contain the excitement I have just to be by your side, in the most gorgeous environment." *Grabs Tyler's hand*

"Let's go, we must walk these floors softly, we must talk in a fashion that speaks subtly, for the tone of our voice can create emotions, we must not talk abruptly, for if we want them to listen we must represent his love for us."

The tones of our choices can create beautiful works of art or cause sources of commotion, the laws of our noises can speak in truth or speak very ugly. For the tugging of good and evil will always stand on our shoulders, we must listen to the good voice to diminish the foul motives. As soldiers prepare for war, we are soldiers who prepare for peace, we are soldiers who sacrifice everything we have been taught, we give in to rescue others before they are robbed by the thief. The water shall surely leak if any corruption fills what the human eye cannot see, for Earth is the perfect example of what our Heavenly Father has created for you and me. Minus the bad, we are living God's kingdom on Earth whether we realize it, or whether we realize who the king is really. We are all spiritual beings whether you are trapped in the logical part of your brain, whether you operate out of the abstract, I am sure you are aware of these dreams. Dreaming with my eyes open is the only way I can see, for when I open my eyes I bring my dreams to reality, I oftentimes catch myself daydreaming but I am conscious of this, so I come back to the present creating what I was just dreaming. See logic will get you from point A to B but imagination will take you anywhere as Einstein believes. He is right for imagination is a gift the human eye can't see, until someone chooses to operate in it, creating the unseen, for every human eye to see. It really is as simple as believing in the power that the creator placed in you and me. For this power is supernatural, it passes the natural, we must have faith in order to understand these things, for if you have the faith of a mustard seed, you can move any mountain as you excel in the direction of the unseen. It is my right to be who I am, it is God's right that I always let him hold my hand, for he knows the way through this life, for I have been lost many times but it is on his rock that I shall stand, even if they mock saying I am just a man. For they do not comprehend, for they shall never understand if they choose to listen to these voices that play on repeat inside their own heads. He rejoices over us with singing, he knows us for who we really are, spiritual beings, he would like to have full control of our decisions, for he knows what is best, and what is best for these people. *Slow piano playing* Stirring up these words as I put them on the pages, stirring up these cages for this is more than just a game, this is more than just a phase, this is the final moment where we can see within range, of who is coming to hurt us and who is coming to save. The synopsis shall surely draw you in, this isn't hypnosis, I am not trying to brainwash you, my friend, this is what is real and what really exists, for the spiritual forces shall always win, for in the distance I can see the enemies retreating as I write with this pen. A child shall lead them, a child shall greet them, a child shall represent the kingdom, a child is more than just a child, we operate out of the figments of our imagination, we concentrate on key points of information that is presented at hand, for I was never programmed by the system, I chose the pill to listen to my heart instead, I chose the choices that created this art, I am compelled where this ink has brought me, it is very compelling these words mean more than what they can spark. Let us love one another, be good to our brothers. Cherish our sisters, respect our misters, write letters for our elders, and come together as one, for in unity we all operate better. The stranger it may seem, we are here for a reason even if we are not sure what that reasoning is, it is a must for us to get more intelligent, for us to discern who our friends are really and who is there to help us. The peace of mind, the pieces of time, the releases of the grind, the condolences that scream for you and me, the raw feelings that will restore all of the signs, this is more than just poetry, this is more than just a moment lived on the ocean, this is the beginning of our existence, this is the hope for all of humanity. Lucy and I walk downstairs in the cavern, down the hallway of intricate paintings, till we arrived in the auditorium.

"It is about time you sleepless souls arose," replied Paul, "we would like to take you up on that offer of riding the unicorns by the crystal sea."

"Yes, of course right this way please." We followed him down the stairwell of many stones, we arrived out in this indescribable image of nature, so many colors we saw before our eyes, oversized butterflies, flew in the air, they had the most beautiful designs, wow I still can't believe this stuff exists, I still can't believe I am here with my wife. Pleasing temperatures, pleasing sights, pleasing wonderful works of nature that bestowed before us, glorious sounds emitted everywhere, for all of creation knew we have arrived.

"The stable is just over there," replied Paul. We were a little nervous to see these creatures much less ride them, but the excitement overpowered the anxiety. *We arrived at the stable*

Paul opened the stable doors, the unicorns were so happy to see us, they marched in place as they were ready to take us for a ride. Colors of purple, blue and white covered these unicorns, a glimmering crystal that was about two feet long had grown on their foreheads.

"Oh my, look at these, Tyler, look at the nature that is crafted right before our own two eyes, such mystery, so much history." We both climbed on the saddle that Paul set up on the unicorns.

"Careful now," replied Paul, "you want to be very gentle with these animals, they can sense your fear. So think happy thoughts and everything shall flow from there." We held the ropes, these instruments controlled the speed of the creatures and the direction we wanted them to go. Paul also gave us a necklace, this was a special unique necklace, and crystals like from the palace covered it. The pendant was a ruby cross.

"When you two are ready to return, hold tight to this cross and it will bring you home."

"Thank you so much for everything, Paul," we both replied.

He led us out of the stable, slapped the unicorns on their butt, on your way now! The air flew through our hair, the ground shook as these creatures were set free with loving care. Galloping, all of the creatures bowed as we made our way through the forest, deer, bears, lions, honoring us. Showing their loyalty and royalty as we traveled this land. Green moss covered these trees, golden glowing apples hung from these apple trees. This was more than an opera scene, we could hear choirs of angels' voices echo as the sound crossed the water on the crystal sea. Blink, Blink, Blink our eyes opened and shut as we witness these things.

"What are you thinking about, Lucy?"

"Since our whole world was shifted, I think about how we are truly connected, I think about the fact that our age may make us young but the experiences have made our souls mature since we were neglected, we have older souls inside of these young bodies, to the external world we are still babies, but in reality we have been here for a while." *Smiles*

"Miracles are real, these emotions can heal. I would like us to have children of our own that we can nurture. I believe that God can heal me and allow me to bear my own children don't you babe?"

"Yes, darling I do believe that. I believe he endowed us with his power that our power goes where we choose, that he will allow us to do all things in love as long as it benefits his kingdom too."

"Since we sought him with all of our heart we found him, he was waiting for us all alone, even flashback to the days when we were all alone. We didn't understand the situation then and what could happen in these poems but he had all the answers, he had all of the songs, he knew all of our wrongs, yet he chose to love us anyway, he chooses this for all of the ones that do and don't belong, for we all belong to him, we all belong, he is with you right now as you read, call on his heavenly name and he shall comfort you in the places that you shall proceed. He shall intercede.

"I would love to have babies with you, I am sure that God will answer our prayers but even if he doesn't, I still love you. I chose you for you. I chose you for the love in your heart. You can make anyone smile when you enter a room, you can inspire creativity in the dark, a beacon of light that is always lit for it creates thoughts. It manifests us as one, it manifests even the sun. It is your heart that captured my heart, it is your spark that sparked my spark, it is your hand in mine, it is your hand that holds my heart, it is your eyes that capture all time, they are the windows to our soul, you are the wind that carries me, as I cry for you to hold me when I am cold. You are the reason that I am alive, everything that you are puts out the fire as the demons roasted me you brought me back to life, it is this thing called love that holds all power, it is something that God placed in all of us, it is the reason for all of us, he loves us all and I love you for everything that you are. I am really grateful that you are my wife. See, writing puts me in my power place, it is through writing that I am able to connect to my higher self, it is through creating with thoughts that I really can create, it is as I crawl through this maze, walking through this cave, chained to my thoughts am I really a slave? Or have I broken the chains experiencing complete freedom, washed in a downpour of grace? I am picking up the microphone, I pray that my stories can capture every soul, I pray that you can see the light on the inside, as I ignite my soul, letting go of my past, letting go of my foes. Forgiving the ones that hurt me, loving myself enough to separate myself from them is essential truth be told, I desire true happiness, as these concepts are unfolding. We gallop into the sunset as it comes down upon us.

"Hey Lucy, there is something over there that catches my eye, let's slow down." We slow down our gallop on the unicorns, and we come to a complete stop.

"Hold on a second babe."

"What is it, Tyler?" I get down from the unicorn helping Lucy get off.

"Lucy, it is sparkling and glowing."

Hundreds of birds fly overhead as we walk toward it, it is purple-colored rose bush that has blue stems instead of green stems. When I picked a rose, huge trees shifted with the dirt, the whole earth was shifting. I gave the rose to Lucy.

"Tyler, look, look over there!" A beautiful log cabin in the woods with a large pond revealed itself to us at this moment.

"I have a genius idea, let's build a bonfire as we examine the stars tonight? How does that sound?"

"I would love that so much babe, we don't have to return, we shall share the sky and the hammocks together."

There is a genius in these genes, there is generosity in these genes. There is a beautiful rhyme scheme that entices the soul as I collect all of my dreams. I had to do it, I had to go through it. I had the volume of skill sets to get through the sewers. I had the options that came along as I write these movies. I had the caution tape wrapped around my whole being, caution because these demons run when I am near because even the son of God recognizes the fact that we are all here, caution because these demons radiate fear for when I call on Jesus these evil spirits shall be killed. These hurt people shall be healed, this earth, these landscapes, and every single hill has an up a down that, is a part of the drill, that is the mark, this soul was found, I have a love affair with creating art, I have the understanding to create, the condensation to create these waves, for the rain may come, see I have a well, it is a wishing well, I drop pennies in it every day, wishing to get out of this hell if I drop quarters in it do you think it may happen faster, do you think I will get rescued or will this end in a disaster? Matter of fact, I am not sure but I am sure of this, there is a reason you and I can still fight, there is a God that restores our soul after every single fight, see the holy one gives all of us wings. The kind that we wear depends on our seeds, what we plant into the lives of others who love everything. See I have angel wings, I choose love over hate, I choose happiness during every single debate, and courage is one of the many talents it takes to be great, believe in yourself, and believe in his name. Lucy and I grab our unicorns and ride to the spot by the pond. This pond is as blue as blue raspberries, it even smells like blue raspberries. We saddle our unicorns to a post, Lucy sits on the log bench as I gather firewood, twenty minutes go by and I am all finished gathering tinder. I douse the wood in lighter fluid, lighting up the darkness that has spread over the country, in an instant, the fire blooms in such a blooming discovery. I sat up the hammock from one tree to the other, as I give kisses to my lover, we climb inside cuddling one another, admiring the stars, which was our company, the beautiful full moon lit up the night sky. Here we are hand in hand, here we are holding promises that came from the desert land, it is so beautiful how we shall never thirst again, we drink upon our Father's water that quenches all of our sins, we swim in his water, and he is our most interesting friend. Lucy and I laugh together, we smile together, we cry together, we frown together, we may not always agree on the same topics, sometimes we may disagree with the weather, Lucy has the most beautiful sweater, she got it from Santa when she was a young woman, when she was just 11, I wonder what it is like to walk the streets of gold up in heaven, I was only seven when I saw my guardian angel. She was dressed in all white, she had the most glorious appearance, it was her love-filled spirit but she looked like you and I. I have fallen in love with these ideas of how Lucy is the one and Lucy is my life. These characters are showing up in my story, I control their thoughts as I create them with my imagery, for

I give them meaning, as you read each word when you read each meaning. I have always wanted to get this story out but I didn't know how to, so I wrote a couple of poems, googled publishing companies, Austin Macauley showed up, then they showed me how to submit my work. Thank you to the team that found all these words out, thank you to the people on the other side who have faith in this route, for this talent is my way out, it is calming to know that I have the stage to impact millions of peoples' lives with my mouth, through intense poetry expressing this loving passion, it is all about attitude. See I am in touch with my sensitivities, I can sense good vibrations through the atmosphere and I can sense bad vibrations, I can sense body language even if their lips are saying different things, I can sense if they truly love me or if they are putting on a front because they are really shady. I can sense when they are talking in other rooms, I can sense what they really mean, if they truly mean well or if they truly are full of deceit, I can discern with the spirit what this human eye can't see, I call it is my sixth sense, it is the holy spirit that lives inside of me. It is his holy presence that holds all the keys, it is my Jesus that shall free us, we are here for a moment and then we shall disappear. Where shall we go? We shall go to a place that is overflowing with love, happiness, and gratitude, surrounded by the most beautiful spirits who operate out of the best attitudes. These beings will not be rude, these creatures are full of kindness, and it is the way that I am paving this map for you. It is the way that I walk down this road, it is the way that our life unfolds, it is the way I shout when I'm close, it is the way that I choose love at all cost, I choose happiness, I choose to carry the cross, I choose victory over every coin toss, it is a price that shall be bought, for I shall never lose this mission or drive I am on, for sometimes I may take a loss, for if I do I shall bounce back, these naysayers can hate, they just mad because they are still late, they still walk in this negative spirit that is a toxic filled plate, they choose to walk with this evil because it is their best friend. I am oh so thankful for every single one of my friends, and how I still fight for them for we all shall win. I find it fascinating how they use to hate, now they are patting me on the back and giving me praise, all because of my talents I was different, all because I was different they wouldn't let me in, all because I just wanted love, all I wanted was some friends, someone to be there to the end, to rescue me from the torment, sheltering me on this land, protecting me from the screams that still bring haunt to this hand, I am thankful for all of my loved ones and friends. It truly is a miracle that my message got through, it truly created ripples in the constitution too, of how to love one another and how to love the outcasts, for we all matter too. Don't let your worries consume you, don't get in a hurry rushing to the next moment, remember to slow down cherishing the moment before you live in the present, think with a level head, unless you are operating out of your imagination, choosing to get out of your own head, choosing to let these words become medicine as you spit them overhead, talking in this mic, my message to be delivered is a about doing what is right, not choosing judgment but choosing to walk with the light, walking with Christ, escaping the devices of evil that try to overtake the night, choose your inner voice, choose: Loyalty, Duty, Respect, Honor, Integrity, Personal Courage. These are the seven army values, let me go into detail. Loyalty, being loyal to who you love, and what you love. Duty, serving at all costs to get these messages across or going after the work that is assigned to you. Respect, treating everyone equally with the same amount of dignity as the next man. Honor, honoring all of the men and women who have come before you, who have changed the way that we see the world. Integrity being honest to yourself, your dreams, your loved ones, your authority, and your country. Personal courage is one of my favorite ones because it takes personal courage to go out there and do something no one has ever done before. It takes personal courage to feel the fear and do it anyway, it takes personal courage to choose to be brave in circumstances that make us afraid. Courage is what separates the boys from men because the boys may not try but the men keep getting up after getting knocked down, chose to always get back up no matter what, people may encourage you to get back up but only you can muster up the courage to believe in yourself, believe in your dreams, getting back up to fight for your team. Belief is a sport, to be honest, those who believe in themselves travel the farthest, those who spread messages of love and happiness have the biggest hearts, those who choose to smile after being bit the hardest, are the real definition of a warrior, determined to hit every target. If you were to ask for my definition of what a champion is, I would tell you that a champion is someone who knows what they want, and what they are willing to give in order to get there. I am the one that shall lead them, I am the one that shall feed them, I am the one that shall be a friend to them, I am just proof of his work, proof of his presence is what is real my friend. These answers that you all seek, you shall unlock as you swim in the depths of these streams in, from different galaxies we are created and different passages we can sense such things, it is from the ashes we love for our spirits shall live for eternity, where we spend it depends on who we call king. There is no other name than Jesus, there are no other chains than can be broken except by his sweetness, he will break your chains if you ask him for strength as you wrestle these demons. Holy is the Lamb of God who sits upon the throne, Holy is the risen king that has sent his son to save us all. All sorts of birds soared in the night, vibrantly colored creatures, red, orange and white, gliding overhead, flying on by, singing praise to the newlyweds, praise to the one on high, praise to this couple whose liberation was a story that was made right, a story of sacrifice, a story of a lot of fights, a story of how good overcame evil, withdrawing my children out of the darkness that filled their lives, I rescued you both and I plan to rescue many more, I plan to break down every evil spirit that operates behind closed doors, I will come for my little children, for it is you that I adore, I am your defender, I am your sword, I am your deliverer, I shall always open the door, I record these events from instinct, these stories I tell are more than a blink, the liquids you consume are more than just a drink, these tales I tell shall surely make you think, of an abstract world created with creativity. See creating is the existence of thoughts that enter into our minds, whether we act upon them is a question better left for the unsaid, but I say always listen to the good voices inside, for these voices come from a world that has never been seen with the human eye, only seen with the eyes of your spirit it is a conclusion that is beyond the skies, beyond the galaxies for it is generated from the heavens, it is recreated in thoughts for us to share. Share with others this creative mind, sharing what it means to truly hurt, what it means to truly cry, what it means to truly love, what it means to truly lift one another as we fly. The simplicity is simple, the complexity is complex, the diversity as these meanings come alive, it's in these verses as I sit in church, I oftentimes catch myself praying, talking to my Father in heaven, I close both of my eyes and open up my third eye, being sensitive to the holy spirit for the spirit shall speak to you, the spirit shall comprehend your cry. The lyrics will represent more than just thoughts, they shall represent the abbreviations from birds to the sky. The personification of the pen that breathes life, I can feel its heartbeat as it is connected to my life. As the waves come and go, as I sit on this raft directing which way to go, directing my soul, as I am conscious of the wind for it knows which direction to blow, as I sit in silence watching everyone panic through life as I am overwhelmingly calm, for the environment may shake us at times, the giants may try to cause an earthquake in our lives, we must remember this, this too shall pass for we will be stronger when we get out alive, we shall be wiser influencing others as we tell about this fight, we shall be lighter as we drop our stories off in this pile, we shall choose love, for it will be different types, ingrained in this tile, for miles and miles we shall walk this journey, sometimes it may be difficult, the real shall separate themselves for we do more than just talk the talk, we hit every target because we were designed to walk the walk. I am in no hurry for I know where I am going, for the ones that matter most shall come to me through encouragement, for I am only 22 years old and I shall suffer no more punishments. I shall light up other people's life, that is my passion, see when I was young, I had to witness those lashes, I pray that my story will influence all of humanity, if you are suffering do not be afraid of the consequences tell someone about it, tell someone at your school about it, tell someone outside of your family, if you have to write it in a letter and drop it off to your school counselor, I know it may be difficult to talk about such things in person but you have to find your way out in order to get rescued. You have to explain these buried emotions in order to get delivered from the evil that may devour you. Be brave, be courageous, and choose a different thought today, for our thoughts shall cause changes. Our changes will be involved with arrangements of how to save these citizens, who are suffering in these cages. I focus on the positive it is the way that I make it through life, time is so fickle yet so amazing, intricately designed we are more than just pages, we are more than just creators, we are centered by our mind, body, and spirit, this love is contagious. This love shall cover all of the nations, I pray that these words make it to all of the places, for these words mean so much more than what they mean as you digest them, as you read them off of these spaces. Making room for all of this love to enter in, making room to become lifelong friends with every friend, changing shoes for all to listen in, for we all have different stories and different ways of letting people in. Different placemats, yet we have this in common, we see with two eyes, we listen with two ears, we walk with two legs, and we hug with two arms, not so different physically if you were to ask me. When it comes to spirituality, there is not one person that is alike, we are all so diverse which allows us to share beautiful ideas, creating spectacular inventions to share, it is so important yet, while we are all so much the same physically, yet so diverse spiritually, to love one another, for love is the greatest teacher, for loving shall heal all wounds, love shall restore us to the right temperature. We must forgive the ones who have hurt us, but never let us forget what it taught us, and never should we feel guilty for disconnecting yourself from their evil, for we must do this to remain pure. This content is soothing for you and me, these moments, I will never forget of you and me, these watches that watch you and me, these contests that cause us to create bringing these words to life, these monsters that roam through the night, are a part of my imagination, they are a part of the disguises, it is where the evil does hide, it is in the graveyards, where good and evil spirits reside, it is between our own two ears that our mind fights for what is right. Lucy and I both fell asleep through the night, we slept stomach to stomach as we hung in this hammock all through the night, I wrapped my arms around this beautiful woman that God surprised me with, yet though it was hard to get past her barrier walls, where she was hiding, she eventually opened up to me and let me inside, she is my best friend and I love her with everything that I am, it is because of her that I pick up this pen and fight. It is my mission to end human suffering for everyone, for I will always protect her and she shall always be just fine, this love is surreal it is more than what meets the eye, it is the mere magician that can cause you and me to fly, it is the pure tragic that happened that caused her and me, to open our hearts to love each other as we continually fight, loving the one that created us, loving our Heavenly Father, he is the lord most high. I find events fascinating that change our life forever, like receiving this contract signing with this publishing company that is in New York City, I am sure they are receiving some cooler weather, I admire the staff, the production, editing, marketing teams that make this work available to people to read, see myself as a young man I am still a leader, I believe in leading them, I believe in achieving all of my goals, for what is a life without goals, a life where we don't stretch ourselves to hit achievements, to change other people's perceptions, to change other people's directions, to get us all on the same page as I write out these inceptions. As I state with this collection, for if we all come together to stand up for what is right, we shall truly represent love, and we shall truly represent the light that the creator placed in you and I. See one Summer, I was a hunter, one hundred people were searching, they came from the land down under, a hunter to be king, a hunter to be a lover, a hunter to represent we are than just blood, we are here to recover, we are here to discover, we are here to go undercover if we must, to reveal the truth, to bring out the concealment of others. See I touch my face, in this body, I am a part of the human race, in this race, we race to the top because we do not want to end up in the last place, the places in these places are aligned with creation, and we are more than just humans who are more than competitive and dangerous. We are beacons of love, we are beacons sent down from above, and see Jesus placed the universe within, as you think, so you shall win. So shall you become one with thoughts for thoughts are very powerful, for thoughts are my friends, sometimes these words can be a mouthful but please understand, this is me breaking down these concepts, revealing a large number of views. As the sun rises, hundreds of birds flew around us, singing beautiful sounds, radiating the light, morning was here and it was clear, I was with the most important one, the one who is dear, hundreds of fish jumped out of the water to greet us as we opened our ears, oh how breathtaking the sunrise was, for the colors that lit up the sky, you would have had to be there it was an amazing sight.

I kissed her lips.

"Good morning, baby."

"Good morning love, I love you thank you for holding me in your arms, protecting me, oh how did I get so lucky by finding you? I have to admit, Lucy, I am the lucky one or maybe we both are very lucky to have one another, I love you."

We kiss some more as I run my fingers through her hair as us two love birds are adored. She sucks on my neck leaving marks on my neck, she calls it marking her territory for short. To be taken by the best is what it feels like to be truly blessed, to be loved by the most beautiful woman, she has the most beautiful hair, and the way her blue eyes twinkle when I get lost in her stare has me longing to look a little while longer as she is obliviated from her fears. She loves and cares for me, I love and care for her, she is the love of my life, the love that I write about. I experience this at this place called Earth with my dear Lucy, she shall no longer hurt. Ever since birth on this planet, we have been hurt, but we choose to represent love, to smile without a cause, to love with everything we are, to love at all costs. The sun rose above the sky, the clouds rose enough to get high, the crowds chose enough support that you could hear

165

them passing by, they examined us in the woods to make sure we were alright, they were our guardians, they were our life, they lived to protect us, they lived to do what is right, as a guardian I take care of my wife, as a pardon, she restores me throughout my life, we complete each other for we bring different gifts to the table, we give different shifts at the stables, we allow lifts to lift us till we are able, we are both two independent connected spirits, who are warriors of the same God. For when I am weak she is my strength, for when she is at her peak I am her source of grace, for when we are in the middle as we run this race, we call on the holy one to give us patience, for we are characters in this fable, we are stars that burn bright, we are the stars of changes, we are the parts of missing cables, for our hearts are joined together, we are able. We are capable to rescue everyone suffering, we hold the labels to release those aren't available, for they pass us by every single day, whether we know it or not, they could be the one who needs the most help, for when they go home, they scream in their room alone by himself, calling on a savior to rescue them from their hell, they need help, this book is to rescue everyone that is in need of someone to shelter them from their self, or shelter them from the monsters that beat on everyone else. It takes someone strong to smile after they have witnessed torturing, it takes someone a long time to heal from the brokenness but when all faith is restored all strength shall be given in multiples from the floors to the ceilings, from the ground to the heavens, we shall be restored in love and truth, we shall be given help from others, we shall be comforted by the creator who created us. I am a messenger of truth, I do not wish to cause disruption on the news, or cause humankind to divide into anger, I come to restore us to who we were created to be, loving spirits here to help each other, it is was my Heavenly Father preached, so let us all come together regardless of our beliefs, let us love one another, let us serve the lowly for they shall lead us out of the valley, for we all have been lonely, but I have carried them close to my heart, whether they realized it was me that was there in that hole. I been here through the good times, the bad times, the great times, and the sad times, I have always been God, for I shall always be God, see Tyler is one of my vessels, I have sent him to be a beacon of light to send out my messages, through his hardships I have given him wisdom and understanding, for I can operate in you all, if you believe in your heart, call on my name, this isn't some voodoo or sorcery, this is the true God that shall deliver everyone from these rages, I shall rescue those that are locked in cages, I shall free those who are willing to make the changes, to be who I created them to be, to love in all places. Lucy and I both got up and out of the hammock, let us go check out this cabin.

We both walked to the door, knocked, someone answered, "Who is there?" a voice came through from the other side.

"It is Tyler and Lucy, we are here on our honeymoon adventure."

Paul requested for us to come here.

"Oh yes, I do remember receiving a letter about the arrival of you two."

This was a tall man, strong muscles, broad chest, big arms, clean shaved with really long hair, he wore a French braid in his hair, his hair was also crimson red, his eyes were

167

green, kind of reminded me of a watermelon with the correspondence of colors.

"I am cooking up some breakfast if you both care to join me."

"We are starving," we replied.

"Great, I am cooking up scrambled eggs, sausage, bacon, and buttered toast."

"That sounds delicious, that will be very feeling, we haven't eaten since we feasted with Paul when we first got here, and it surprised us to because we really weren't that hungry yesterday but today we were feeling it."

"My name is Jacob, I forgot to mention, and I am very excited to have visitors, for visitors are very few nowadays."

"Why do you say that?" I replied.

"See with so much darkness in the world, only a few represent the light, therefore, secluding us from reality, therefore removing us from their mentality. You and Lucy are very special unique beings, Jesus touched you both when he brought you here, Jesus knew the suffering you two would endure and how his name would be made famous as you strived to find the cure, for the cure is love, as you two are, the hope for humanity is carried on the shoulders of these two love birds. You both will influence millions of people, for happiness shall defeat all of the evil, causing it to retreat in the mist, retreating into the puddles. For his holy love is a witness to host, his holy presence is the holy ghost, for the holy ghost resides in you both, for you tapped into the spiritual realm, as you walked this earth, for many people may not understand or comprehend your souls, but it is the lord of hosts who knows your heart is the holy ghost.

168

Please sit down at our table." *reaches out his hands to us both*

"Will you pray with me?"

"Yes we shall pray with you." Lucy and I both bow our heads.

"Dear Heavenly Father we come to you, into your never-ending love for us, I am very thankful for the opportunity to commune with these found souls, the missionaries who tapped into your soul, I pray that you will protect them from anyone who shall come against them, I pray that you will always be their best friend, I pray for the lost ones who have not been found in your love, I pray that you shall rescue them all, I pray for the safety, for everything lately, it's been a little crazy, you know the reason for what you are doing, you are the safe key. I pray that you bless this food to our bodies as we fellowship together, I pray that you will restore every person reading this, I want them to know, and they are my babies, amen."

"Look at all of this scrumptious food Lucy. It smells so good. I can't wait for the first bite. Yummy, it hits the spot. It is savory enough to warm our hearts. It is tasty enough to capture this moment."

It is amazing how we can connect when we eat, it is always a special time when we can come together from all of the hectic things, we encounter in life, to sit down at peace right by the fire, to enjoy this breakfast, to talk about our lives, to talk about the chapters we are in, to exchange information of things we are encountering, as we walk this road as we journey through time. The prosperity that comes to the prosperous, the abundance that comes to the abundant, the excitement that fills the excited, while the gratitude increase with grace, the wisdom that I give to the wise, these definitions are no longer stuck in place, these are values we embrace, for they connect us all, they connect our spirits in the human race. I aim to teach valuable information as I inform you all, I aim to be more than just a man, and I pray to let you all witness the spirit in my soul. We cannot heal in the same environment that destroyed us, we cannot grow in soil that contains no nutrients, we cannot grow in the places where the toxins do flow, we cannot love if we are consumed with hate, we are frozen, we cannot move, we must call on the holy one to move, to melt the ice allowing us to get out of the waves that come to destroy, for there is still time we can all be rescued, we can all grow beautifully in new soil, we can all eat delicious food as the pot boils, we can all have clothing that warms us from the cold, we can all live lives of satisfaction, not regretting a single thing when we are old, for we may make mistakes sometimes, no we are not perfect but it is our desire to be our best, it is our desire to love everyone like the rest, it is our desire to reflect on the oppressed, to breathe life into the depressed, for we are all here for a reason, do me a favor, put your hand on your chest, can you feel that beat, can you feel your heartbeat at rest, for that is the purpose that I place inside of your chest, that is the service that emits from your head, for with these thoughts you can hear over there, for these thoughts are here and these thoughts are aware. For the ones in foster care, the ones that have no remembrance of their parents, I hate it, that you have to be in there, but it is safer in their arms than to be lost in the jungle, alone out there, learn as much as you possibly can, impact generations, see I impact from where I stand, loving my friends separating myself from the enemies, exiling all forms of hate. I am coming together with the love, reaching for the surface, reaching for the turtle doves, climbing this ladder so I can reach what's above, expanding my imagination as I numb the hurt, for love covers all wounds, love is an emotion that my Father created when he chose us. Oh, how magical this existence is, oh how tactical our feelings exist, oh how elastic, what is real and what isn't for it exists, for things not seen with the eye are the most real. Success can be scary at times, but I would much rather be scared and successful, than scared and broken. Do not be overwhelmed with thoughts, no matter where you are, don't let what's inside paralyze you, preventing you not to act at all for we can generate power, we can achieve where we put our minds, everything we need is inside of us, we must believe in the possibilities, for when you are about to, you will witness miracles, for all of your doubts shall be diminished, never allow them to keep you stuck inside, for you shall experience the most satisfying life, you shall be doubt proof. After Lucy and I finished eating with Jacob, we brush our teeth, showered, changed our clothes, and then figured out what adventure we shall tackle this afternoon.

"Hey Lucy, Tyler, I have a boat if you two would like to go fishing together, you both are more than welcome to relax on the water, it is very peaceful fishing."

"That sounds amazing Jacob, we would love to fish as a couple, but we also are on this journey, kind of excited to see what the next place holds for us. Thank you so much Jacob for catering to us, providing us with a delicious meal, providing us with a friendship that can never be stolen, thank for being our friend, thank you for the notions. Thank you for making us welcome in your home, thank you again for the food it was so delightful."

Lucy and I both went outside after taking care of our personal hygiene. I envied her when she walked, I envied her when she talked, I envied her when she spoke, I envied her for she was my rose, such a beautiful creature that I got the opportunity to grow with, she had the perfect shape when she walked, she had the perfect ways most of all, oh how her eyes captured my soul, oh how her beautifully she existed, oh how she captured the stars, for when she was with me gravity had no effect on me, for I floated away with her for we floated into our dreams, we floated pass the sea, we floated past the green, we were glowing beyond the blue, we were wonderful works of art that could not be described, we were seagulls waiting to fly, we were deep sea divers waiting to dive, we were more as we spoke, we were more as we came alive, we were adored by each other, we were adored by life, we meant more to each other than your typical husband and wife, we took care of each other, we were more than what we knew we were more than what we cried, we were more as we opened our arms up wide, we were lovers who loved, fighters who fight, we were the definition of unconditional love, having eternal life, having eternal rights, rescuing these lost souls out of the darkness at night, rescuing these puppets on strings who were looking to make things right, we wanted to just be who we really are, we wanted the freedom to not be blind, I took Lucy's hand, there was a commotion as we drunk these healing potions, it was Jacob he was causing a ruckus, we were alarmed but it was simply him starting up the circus. Animals of all kinds freely roaming in a tent, for these creatures were all tamed, they would not hurt a hand, and they rubbed against our waist, showing us affection for we were there friends.

"These are my pets, these are my friends, for each and every single one of these animals can do tricks, they are full of talent, they can do handstands. I host multiple shows for the residents here ever so often."

"That is really neat. Jacob," I replied. These descriptions are descriptive, these conditionings are conditions, these words can mean so many different things, and it just depends on the position. Far from here, far is clear, far is near, far ahead, oh how amazing it is to be far away from there, far from the places that caused so much dread.

"Tyler look at me, what do you see?"

"I see a beautiful angel with the most breathtaking wings, for you may not know it but you are the one I need, you are always on my mind even when I wake up from my dreams, I sing of you when I close my eyes to breathe."

"Before you two leave, I have something to say, don't forget who you are as you journey through this place, don't lose that spirit that the good lord placed in you, as long as you take care of others, your Father will take care of your life, always love your brothers, always love your wife, always love others, always radiate his light, for this life is fragile, it can be shallow, for in the depths of the deadly shadows, call on the light. Tyler, God sent you your beautiful wife, you must treasure her above all else, you must treasure her with your life, you must provide, keeping her warm from the cold as you hold her in your arms, as you both are covered with blankets inside. For the fire shall keep you two warm as it rains outside, share your talents together, you shall feed her when she is hungry, for you two are a team, when one of you is sick you shall be there for one another, you have all that you need, two hands to help, two feet to walk, a set of lips to speak, and a tongue to talk. For from your mouth flows the riches of life, you can restore lost souls or cut people like a knife, yet so small it is very powerful, for the words you speak can be delightful, so can the seeds you plant as you are out in this vast green land, for the harvest shall be plentiful, for those that labor with their hands, shall reap all of their desires, they shall always have a place on our Father's land. This is my last sentence to you both until we meet again, safe travels for you both, I now have two new friends."

So on our voyage we went, Lucy and I both got on our unicorns, galloping through the forest of vivid colors so bright, this way Lucy we took a right, we still have crystal seas to see.

"Look at all those butterflies, Tyler, oh how magical, look at those fairies flying through the air, flying circles around us." Cupid appeared out of nowhere, shot these two lovers, creating an aura of love that radiated from the both of us.

"I love you, Tyler. I have enjoyed every moment being by your side."

"I feel the same towards you, my dear, I love you too."

We both continued to ride, we could see the vast blue waters up ahead, crystals surrounded the crystal sea, a vast, blue body of water was painted on the land for all of creation to see.

"Would you like to go for a swim, Lucy?"

"Yes love, good thing we packed our swimming gear, there is a patio bench with an awning over there, let's saddle the unicorns up there." Being real, being humble, and being kind are three characteristics that are most important that we should all carry as we journey through life.

"Sounds great, Lucy."

We both get down from our unicorns and tie their ropes to the post. We both get undressed getting in our swimsuits.

"You look very gorgeous in your suit, babe."

Her two-piece was very magical. It was covered in purple and white flowers. My swimsuit was very angelic, white feathers with a gold metal piece that went around my waist. I watched her get in the water, it was so divine, the way her breasts and boobs were shaped, I couldn't get my eyes off of her. Her behind was a beautiful sight, and the best part is that she is all of mine.

"His wide chest, his strong arms, the way you could see the definition of his back and core. Come here baby, I am so grateful that you are all of mine."

We both wrapped arms in the water, rainbows appeared all over the sky when we were joined together, we kissed, we held each other, we were in love, and she is the love of my life. She ran her fingers up my face, holding me by my jawline as she sucked on my bottom lip pulling away as she came back to kiss me some more, she wrapped her legs around me as I took her top off because she didn't need it anymore. I kissed down her neck, I kissed on her breasts, and we passionately loved on each other embracing each other for everything we are. We made love in the water, we poured out our love for one another, we comforted each other, and we are infatuated lovers.

"I will love you no matter what. I will be the one that feels you, for when you forget how to touch, I will care for you throughout the rush, that leaves us high for days, high off of each other's love, I will hold you in my arms for eternity, you will be captured in my heart, till we both pass out or leave, we will sail together on a raft as we crossover into different dreams, we will lead each other for we both agree, we will always be driven by the passion-filled love we express in our rings."

They both glowed blue and red when we are together.

"I can feel your pulse in mine just as you can feel my pulse in yours, so no matter where we are, for if we are apart, we will have the security in knowing that we are still alive."

We both laid upon our back floating in the water as we held hands, we examined all the beauties of Mother Earth, her creatures, her forestry, her green that encompassed all of creation, her blues that were revealed if forms of water, or the form of the sky. This world is so beautiful, why must people destroy it? Why can't we do what we can to protect her, for she protects us, without it alive, we will not be alive. We must continue to fight the fight to reduce pollution, we must do what we can to save Mother Earth's life, why must others litter, throwing trash out just to get it out of their possession, that is no way to treat the planet that God created for you and I. I pray we all come together to rescue, restore, rejuvenate life, back towards people, back towards our environment, it makes me sad to think about all of God's beautiful creatures swimming in the ocean, dying from us pouring trash into the commotion, we are killing each other and we are killing the creatures God

176

created…Let us choose the greenway, let us cut down on all the pollution that is killing, I am representing the green wave, for the greenway saves everyone, producing life so we can all be okay, this is a revolution I am revealing to your eyes, a revelation of love and happiness I am screaming with my cries. It is never alright to destroy this planet, that produces so much life, I come as one but I stand as 10,000 as I fight this fight, I love my planet, I love all forms of life, let us do the right thing, let us love even if it means to sacrifice. For in sacrifice it creates the atmosphere for miracles to occur. Have you ever experienced a miracle? Have you ever experienced something supernatural? I have, I have had many spiritual events take place in my life like hearing angels sing, being blessed with money when I had no food to eat, our Father shall always provide for his children, if you seek him with all your heart you will find him, delight in him and he will give you the desires of your heart, for it is him who gave you those desires. I can reach people in ways other people can't, you can reach people in ways that I can't, and together we can reach everyone and hit every milestone that needs to be met. Do you hear what I am saying? Do you understand the meaning behind these messages I am sending? Can you comprehend these phases, can you search within yourself to do what is right to save humanity? I sacrifice when I write, I step outside of this human mind that keeps me alive, I step into the spiritual, bringing these topics out to the light, shining a flashlight on them, can you see them now? Will you please join me in this fight? To represent peace, love, and humility, you will not regret your life, for when it is our time to go, we will cross over satisfied with the concepts we wrestle with, the topics that created the sweetest fruits in life.

"Hey Tyler, look over there, hundreds of cats appeared out of nowhere near the unicorns."

We both got out of the water, dried off, all we could hear was meowing coming from the kitties. Meow, Meow, Meow.

"These cats are so adorable, babe."

"They are Tyler, cats bring me so much happiness."

We both laid down in fields of flowers, as these cats climbed all over us. We held them in our arms, furry creatures of love, you could hear them purring as they swarmed us. They were taking their paws and massaging us, I call it making biscuits, they were showing us so much love, Lucy and I rolled around with these kitties. Could this moment last forever, I questioned myself. You could feel the breeze blowing over us.

"I take it you have discovered my cats," a voice came out of nowhere.

"Yes we are in love with them. We both have cats back home. They are our favorite house animal. This woman was very joyful.

"Go on ahead bask in their affection, they love meeting new people."

"That is very kind of you ma'am."

"Have you two heard about the train that has no conductor?"

"No, we have not," we replied.

"Up the mountain, the station awaits the both of you. Once you enter, the door shall shut taking you to the next destination, and it is quite magical if you ask me."

"Where will it take us?"

"That is a secret, you must take the leap of faith, knowing, in the end, you shall be okay."

"It was nice meeting you. Thank you for all of your help," we replied.

Quickly we got on our unicorns, galloped up the trail, that lead us to the top of the mountain. It took us roughly ten minutes to make it to the top. When we arrived, this train station was none like we had seen before. It was a fair-sized train station. You could see the railroad tracks, the cobblestones that we walked on shifted with every step. We walked up the stairs, vines and flowers were growing everywhere, with exotic gems that revealed themselves underneath the nature that was growing. You could feel the energy all over your skin, this was a magical place, full of magical things, full of spiritual seasons, full of creative dreams. It was time to go, Lucy and I both boarded the train, the door shut behind us. We overheard a voice on the speaker, your voyage awaits, for when you arrive, you will be feeling great, for on the other side is a beautiful place, where you two lovers can fully embrace, all of the beauties of the Mother Earth, all of the beauties of this wondrous place. Music filled the air, choirs of angels appeared out of nowhere. Spiritual beings entertained us as Lucy and I sat in this booth. I wrapped her in my arms. She was looking very gorgeous too.

"Aren't you kind of anxious?" I asked her.

She replied, "Yes I am dear but everything has been amazing so far and it can only get better. Everything was created for him and by him so that we may experience what our Heavenly Father experiences."

We held each other in arms as we looked out the window on this train, we held each other as we examined the rain. We were crossing passages of water. We were riding through passages of forests. Oh, how grateful I am for this woman in my life. She was the hope that diminished all of the fires. She was the rope, I held onto through all of these years. She is the ransom for all of these tears, for she covers me in her love and I cover her with my mirrors. I mirror the same love she gives me. I am compassionate about her, and she is the passion that allows me to keep the distance close. Oh, how poetry can come to life when the right composer can be exposed to this pen, with these memories of the future, for we are creating it in the present flight. There was a refrigerator with beverages and food on this ride, there also was an oven. I cooked both of us a pizza. I poured Lucy and me a glass of wine. As we enjoyed the savory deliciousness of this pizza, I could swear it was created by the lord most high. Pepperoni, banana peppers, grilled chicken, green peppers, loads of cheese and red sauce. Mmmm, the smells filled the aroma in the room. We both drank wine as we chowed down on this delicious food. Enjoying the best moments, enjoying the best views, tasting the scrumptiousness that was on our tongues, escaping reality is what we were doing. We were on the honeymoon of a lifetime, for the honey and the moon came together creating our lifeline. This was the most authentic way of living, the most holistic way of understanding what we were really doing. After we finished eating we soon began to get drowsy. luckily, there were more than just benches on this train, and there were comfy couches. Lucy and I both laid down on this huge couch that had memory foam in it. It was so comfy, the temperature was perfect. I couldn't ask for more, I was just a little thirsty, I drank a little bit more as the journey continued to unfold. Lucy wrapped her arms around me as sleep took us over, such peacefulness was our true discovery of us two lovers who were more than just thunder…For when we were together there was a calmness that emitted from our minds, there was happiness like no other, the kind that is hard to find. Sleep fell upon us both. We slept like babies at birth. The train ride was very smooth, with no bumps or sharp turns, all of the walls were a soundproof barrier, so no external noise entered inside. The raw emotion felt in this story really is alive. This fantasy romance I create comes straight from inside my mind. It is my imagination that allows me to create such things, you can create too. I believe in you, don't be afraid, try it and you shall amaze yourself at the things that you do. After three or four hours, we both woke up. We haven't arrived at our destination. I was really craving some marijuana. I could smell it but I didn't know where it was at.

"Hey, babe do you smell that?"

"Yes, Tyler I do. Are you thinking what I'm thinking?"

"Yes, love, I am."

We both searched the interior of the train it didn't take us long to find it, there were perfectly rolled blunts waiting to take us to cloud 9. There was even a decorative lighter, we both lit one up individually, smoking and toking away, getting faded with the smoke, getting relaxed. It is always best waking up from a wonderful nap, lighting a beautiful rolled wrap full of greenery, we were hallucinating in the most joyful loving scenery, smiling from ear to ear, witnessing all sorts of greenery. Thank you Lord for your green, we shall use your herbs as meat, for the green shall lift us up from our feet. We were floating as we loafed in the streets, we were faded as we coughed on the smoke, we were shaking from the tokes, we were sailing huge ships on a vast blue ocean. There were hundreds of deer roaming in green pastures, there was smoke that covered the icy mountains, there were birds flying from all directions, there were many rainbows providing protection, the leaves of the trees were a mixture of yellow, red, and green, what a jaw dropping sight to see, the rivers were blue, the crystals ranged from clear, to purple, to gold, to maroon, oh what a magical world we live in, oh how the magic allows us to look forward to the new, it allows us to step out of our comfort, for in comfort we must appreciate our surroundings, but we must go where no man has gone in order to reveal what is missing in our generation, the lyrics that are missing in so many songs, the tickets that take us places can often be costly, the most valuable currency of all is the effect we have on others for we can inspire or tear down, we can breathe life or breathe death, we can restore what is broken or we can continue to cause breakage, the power is within us we must come to consciousness, to destroy the evil that haunts all men for the power of love shall restore all of the generations. We all truly want to have fun, we want to be entertained by artists that understand the components of gifts, that we all come from, for it is the gifts that make us, it is in the giving that he created in us, so I give my best work so you all can be amazed, for I am just a vessel on this journey through life, listening to my intuition, following my ambitions, letting go of my fears, making the transition, giving in to love, for we are all a part of this realm. We are all a part of this family, we are all searching for connections, we are all yearning for protection, we are all learning through our expressions, we are all intelligent, we all have the power to make the most influential changes. We can all take this bull by the horns, we can all stand together as one, choosing to love all of humanity, creating a movement that is being created in these pages. Creating the tunes, that vibrate through our ages, choosing love no matter what race, choosing love no matter what religion, let us not allow these programs to separate us, for that is what fuels the enemy's fire, putting us all in cages. If you get any message I am relaying, I pray that you choose love, I pray that you separate yourself from any evil that tries to steal your happiness, for peace of mind is vital in being happy. For you shall be truly awakened when you choose love and not hate. Lucy and I held each other, we loved and kissed on each other, if you are getting annoyed at our romance, I will not apologize, it is just something that happens when you fall in love with someone, you give them all of your good things and you give them the bad, for you both work together to prevent sadness, it becomes your role to take care of them, their soul becomes a part of your soul no matter where you are, them being happy, is most important for every relationship is tested some days, but it is the couples that hold on through the hardships and rain, who experience love more abundantly, loving through all of the pain, loving through the sunshine that comes and loving through the rain clouds that appear, you never can tell what the day will be like but if you choose acceptance, understanding from their perspective, agreeing with them even if sometimes you feel rejected. You must put your pride aside if you want to make it last, for don't let a flat ruin your life, if you have to call for marriage counseling to fix the flat then do that, or resolve the conflict together for you both are made to find solutions to the problems, choosing forgiveness and love wrapping each with open arms. The train was slowing down, we were arriving at our destination, we both jumped out of our seats in excitement, we are here baby. The door opened and we made a run for it, before our eyes we were captivated by our sight. This was a huge city that had stone walls going around it.

A servant came to us, "Right this way, King Tyler and Queen Lucy. My name is Kyle, you two have a special appointment."

We climbed into the back of a carriage, thousands of people lined up on the streets, throwing flowers at our feet, welcoming us with love, welcoming us with the most beautiful greetings, the buildings were crafted with stones, gold, and silver, welcome signs were posted everywhere.

"This is quite amazing, Lucy"

"It is Tyler. Who would have thought you and I would be treated with so much royalty, loyalty, and love from others as we simply stayed true to ourselves, we stayed true to what we liked. I love you, Tyler."

"I love you too, Lucy," I replied with a smile.

Many people blew us kisses, bowed to us. We replied with kind gestures as well, blowing them kisses giving love away as they were showing love to us. We arrived at the castle at the top of the city, Kyle helped us get down, we both entered into the palace, the sculptures, and painting that were everywhere captured our eyes. Paul was here, one last thing before you two depart to your homeland, I will crown you King and Queen.

He took the crowns in his hand, placing them on our heads.

"I am so grateful that you and I had the opportunity to meet, this means the world to me. I am so thankful, you followed your dreams, for listening to the voices that came from your Father above, had you both in for a treat. Anytime you want to visit these magical lands, you have that necklace that I gave the both of you, just press the gem and you shall be here in a jiffy. I love you both, king and queen. You have taught us so much. You have represented all of the creation, how to love without hesitation, how to show the exact demonstrations of true character. The exact beings that he created for creation, the both of you stayed true to your angels, I love you all, in blink, you shall be home in your castle, away from this far away land, you both are outstanding."

We hugged Paul and replied, "We are ready."

He sent us on our way. He sent us into our familiar places. We were back in our home in this beautiful kingdom we created, of love, peace, and harmony. It was amazing. Since we were back, we unpacked our belongings, we took a shower, our butler cooked us a hot meal. I haven't mentioned it since our marriage ceremony, but our butler took care of the versions of us that we rescued in the time machine. The children were happy that we were back. We hugged them. We sat down and ate with them, we were all a family. We all shared our love and smiles with one another. What an adventure it has been, what a journey it has been with this pen, it has been exhausting at times but that what happens when you stretch yourself, that is what happens when you pour out your intelligence. I love you all remember to choose love most of all, don't pass judgment for there is one that will judge us all, let us accept each other, for love covers all.